CANADIAN POPULATION AND NORTHERN COLONIZATION

LA POPULATION CANADIENNE ET LA COLONISATION DU GRAND NORD

In their annual sessions the various Sections of the Royal Society are accustomed to take up for general discussion a topic of current interest and this gives Fellows and special guests from the natural sciences, the social sciences and the humanities an opportunity for useful communication across the disciplines on an important subject.

In 1961 the topic was an especially vital issue, the population explosion, and this volume, based on the papers given at the meeting, has much valuable information and many pertinent and provocative comments on this phenomenon particularly as it affects Canada.

T. W. M. Cameron leads off with a general background on the causes and consequences of the population increase around the world. Then come a group of papers presenting various aspects of the population in Canada's settled areas. The second part of the book turns to those largely unsettled areas stretching away in Canada's north and considers the potentialities of these areas as a more permanent habitat for man. With an introduction by Rene Pomerleau, various problems of settlement are brought forward. All these authors stress that any planning for a northern future "must be based on a broad, systematic and thorough scientific appraisal."

This is an important and absorbing book and it will give both specialist and general reader much to think about.

Royal Society of Canada "Studia Varia" Series, no. 8

v. w. BLADEN, the Editor of the volume, whose preface offers reflections on the world problem of population, is Dean of Arts and Science and Professor of Political Economy in the University of Toronto.

ROYAL SOCIETY OF CANADA
"STUDIA VARIA" SERIES

Canadian Population and Northern Colonization

Symposium presented to the
ROYAL SOCIETY OF CANADA
in 1961

La Population canadienne et la colonisation du Grand Nord

Colloque présenté à la
SOCIÉTÉ ROYALE DU CANADA
en 1961

EDITED BY

V. W. BLADEN, F.R.S.C.

PUBLISHED FOR THE SOCIETY

BY UNIVERSITY OF TORONTO PRESS

1962

FINANCIAL ASSISTANCE FROM THE CANADA COUN-
CIL TOWARDS THE PUBLICATION OF THE STUDIA
VARIA SERIES IS GRATEFULLY ACKNOWLEDGED BY
THE ROYAL SOCIETY OF CANADA. THE FACT THAT
A GRANT HAS BEEN MADE DOES NOT IMPLY, HOW-
EVER, THAT THE CANADA COUNCIL ENDORSES OR
IS RESPONSIBLE FOR THE STATEMENTS OR VIEWS
EXPRESSED IN THE PARTICULAR VOLUMES

PREFACE

AN ECONOMIST EDITING this volume of essays is under severe temptation to add another essay under the guise of a preface. Restrictions of space prevent any serious yielding to this temptation, but within the bounds of a few hundred words I propose to make some comments on the world problem of population.

As Dr. Keyfitz shows (p. 36), there are three groups of countries which, from the point of view of population, must be distinguished: a group with no population problem (unless it be that of prospective population decline); a group of wealthy countries with rapidly increasing population resulting from a rise in fertility after a period of decline; and a group of poor countries with very rapidly increasing population resulting from a rapid decline in mortality while fertility remains high. Canada is in the second group, but we have responsibilities to the third group.

The dramatic "explosion" in the *tiers monde* has precipitated much pessimistic writing. "Must we starve?" is a typical title. That the "explosion" presents great problems is not in doubt, but it is too early to panic. We must not simply project growth on the basis of current fertility and of a continued decline in mortality; nor should we ignore the effect on productivity of the rapid spread of developed technology into the lands of growing population. Can we not expect a gradual readjustment of fertility to the new low level of mortality in the newly industrializing countries similar to that experienced in the older industrialized countries? Can we not expect this adjustment to be the result of urbanization and industrialization, of the development of opportunity and the emergence of hope, and of the emancipation of women? This last item I believe to be of crucial importance. Surely the question is not whether we must starve, but rather whether the nations of the *tiers monde* can achieve a satisfactory "take off" for economic development in spite of this rapid population increase.

"Take off" for development requires saving. But saving is difficult in a country of low income; still more difficult if consumption in the form of large families is high; and a high level of saving is necessary where population is increasing if the stock of capital is merely to keep pace with such growth. Barbara Ward in her talks on the Canadian

Broadcasting Corporation ("The Rich Nations and the Poor Nations") quoted an estimate that a 3 per cent annual increase in population required that 9 per cent of the national income be saved if the per capita production is to be maintained. J. J. Spengler, in his article on the "Aesthetics of Population" (*Population Bulletin*, June 1957), estimated that for the United States the percentage of national income that must be saved merely to offset population growth and maintain productivity was four or five times the percentage rate of population growth. This means levels of saving which are hard to expect in the less developed countries where income is low and where the habits of saving and investment and the institutions of the capital market have to be developed. They are levels of saving which are high for the wealthier countries; and these wealthier countries should provide some of the capital required for development of the poorer countries.

It was in conditions of similar worry and pessimism that Malthus wrote his *Essay on Population*. Two questions are suggested to the modern economist when he reads the *Essay* and contemplates the contemporary world. First, with reference to the wealthy countries with high fertility, he may well ask, as Dr. Spengler does, whether parents should not be required "to meet nearly all the costs of procreating and rearing children, costs which at present are being shifted in considerable part to others." This assumes greater significance if one considers the "external diseconomies" of consumption in the form of large families. Second, with reference to the poorer countries with high fertility, he may ask whether external aid, like poor relief in the England of Malthus, may simply postpone the necessary adjustment in the birth rate. But perhaps it was John Stuart Mill who saw the answer to this in his day and ours. He saw that relief (or aid) must be on a massive scale to permit the dawn of hope. We have to make, if this is correct, a very difficult choice of those countries that are to be given this chance. A little aid to many countries may help none of them; massive aid to a few, carefully selected as most likely to "take off," may enable them to "take off." The others must wait; but will they without, in their exasperation and frustration, doing injury to themselves and us?

The essays which follow were read at sessions of the Royal Society of Canada in June 1961. Like the earlier volumes of *Studia Varia*, this volume is evidence of a growing desire of natural scientists, social scientists, and humanists to find common ground and re-establish communication. This, to my mind, is healthy. Of the content of the papers I shall say nothing; good wine needs no bush; and, anyway, I have used up the allotted space for another purpose! I shall simply express my hope that the Society in similar joint sessions will discuss some of the economic, political, social, technological, and cultural problems of the newly developing countries and will consider very seriously the responsibility of Canada to give assistance and the means by which we may most effectively assist these nations.

V. W. BLADEN

CONTENTS

PART I: CANADIAN DEMOGRAPHY

CAUSES AND CONSEQUENCES OF THE
POPULATION INCREASE

Thomas W. M. Cameron, F.R.S.C.

PERHAPS THE MOST IMPORTANT CONSEQUENCE of the establishment of Evolution as a doctrine was the acceptance of man as a member of the animal kingdom—a rather recent and somewhat primitive mammal, both physiologically and physically, with, however, a great development of its brain. This gave man a mental advantage because of the extent of his intelligence and his ability to communicate with his fellows. Nevertheless, he has remained biological rather than logical in his actions and he is guided much more by instinct than by reason. Thinking for most men is at best an intermittent process and is employed only under stress. He is much less rational than he believes himself to be, and the two ruling motives in his behaviour are pain and pleasure. To the great majority of mankind, material and non-intellectual pursuits have always predominated and probably always will.

In his origins, man was an unsocial creature who lived in small family groups until the need for assistance in hunting and in overcoming his innate helplessness forced him to expand into larger units. He is still not really a social animal and he is still very much at the mercy of the conflicting effects of instinct and of reason—and instinct almost always predominates.

The tribal units have enlarged and the populations they constitute can be studied in the same way as the populations of other animals. All, whether man or beast or bird, follow an almost identical pattern.

In any given environment in which suitable foodstuffs exist, the population increases in numbers. The rise is slow at first but it becomes faster and faster until, as the result of a variety of causes—predators, disease, food shortage—it gradually levels off at a density which represents a state of equilibrium. The increase in population, plotted as a graph against time, shows an S-shaped curve in which there are, of course, numerous small irregularities. The upper arm of the S tends to continue for long periods at the same general level, unless some catastrophic event disturbs it. In this case, if the population has not been exterminated, the sigmoid curve starts again, quite often with the population somewhat changed in character. This kind of expansion was at the base of the thoughts expressed nearly two hundred years ago by Brückner and Malthus, who were considering the same problem, although on a much smaller scale, as the one we are discussing here.

Man began his evolution as a nomad hunter and a collector of wild grasses. When he found how to tame some animals and grow grasses, he became an agriculturist. The first settlements and the first tribes were thus created; numbers began to increase and the curve of human populations began to move upwards. As man's efforts at animal husbandry and agriculture improved, some individuals were released from the soil and became urbanized. These still had to be fed and clothed, of course, and as numbers of the non-agriculturists increased, demands on the soil correspondingly increased, so that it gradually lost its original fertility.

The settlements had to put part of their wealth back into the soil to restore and increase its production. The population curve continued to soar geometrically. Man had commenced his interference with Natural Selection. Science came to the aid of his earlier efforts and showed him how to increase food production to an abnormal extent, enabling more and more people to live on the fruits of fewer and fewer. Urbanization increased. The town worker became industrialized and produced material goods which increased the physical well-being of the population, and later—often after catastrophic epidemics of disease— he was able to devote some of this wealth to the prosecution of health. There is, however, a limit to the amount of usable wealth which can be created; production becomes restricted and fails to support the increasing expense of fertilizing the land which again loses its fertility. Numbers are approaching the point where the curve starts to flatten out.

The world still consists of many individual populations, all of them at different levels of development. The primitive lands of Africa with their poor soils and increasing peoples are still in the first stage. Those of the temperate world are on the upward slope of the curve; western Europe is probably highest, with North America not far behind and quite closely followed by the U.S.S.R. The old civilizations of the subtropical belt—southern Europe, northern Africa, and southeast Asia —are approaching the phase when the land is again losing its fertility and the curve is beginning to flatten out. The hungry states are those at the bottom and top of the sigmoid curve.

Everywhere in the world, however, the people are still increasing in numbers, and this again, is due to man's attempted revocation of the Law of Nature which requires the Survival of the Fittest. This law operates through disease and parasites, through hunger, and through selective breeding, and keeps the population at the level consistent with normal health and well-being. Man is altering it with his domestic plants, with his domestic animals and, above all, with himself—mostly himself. The consequence of breaking this law has always been the extinction of the species. Only man has dared to defy it but not even he has been able to repeal it.

Nature deals with the species and is careless of the individual; man, who is less wise than the Nature he has partially supplanted, deals with the individual and is careless of the species.

It is difficult to comprehend the enormous revolution in public health which took place during the first half of this century. Although no infectious disease has as yet been eradicated, many have become exceedingly rare and most others are in process of control. In the temperate parts of the world, diphtheria, typhoid, louse-carried typhus, and relapsing fever are almost unknown. Yet during World War I the louse-carried diseases alone killed several million people. Smallpox also has almost gone and so has plague, while tuberculosis has been steadily declining and, but for wars, would probably be as rare as the others.

The greatest advances, however, were in the tropical lands. Malaria, sleeping sickness, yellow fever, cholera, schistosomiasis, and hookworm disease began to be subject to control. Many of these are epidemic killing diseases but many also are endemic debilitating diseases which lower life expectancy, enfeeble the patient, reduce his working potential, and render him subject to numerous non-specific conditions. The effects of these advances on infant mortality have been striking, although faulty feeding still takes its very considerable toll.

It is, perhaps, important to note that the increase in life expectancy in the tropics was mainly, if not entirely, due to colonial administration which not only prevented tribal warfare but also undertook the control and prevention of both the debilitating and the killing diseases. Colonialism more than all other factors is responsible for the population pressures in the so-called under-developed lands.

In the more advanced communities with their higher standard of living, social responsibility, and family planning, there is a tendency to limit the birthrate. In reasonably healthy unsophisticated primitive communities, however, the crude birth rate is about fifty per thousand. Because of the relative absence of serious disease and the continual excess of children who survive, the crude death rate is about eight to ten per thousand. It follows that, if this rate continues, these communities will double themselves every twenty to thirty years.

By the end of this century the population of the world will have increased from its present 3,000 millions to about 5,000 millions. It is a sobering thought to realize that the human beings now alive represent about 3 per cent of all who have ever lived. It is equally sobering to realize that a high reproductive rate gives any particular population a greater survival potential than a population which has a restricted one.

Prevention of disease is still far from complete, however spectacular the results have been so far, but in the under-developed countries preventive medicine has outstripped improved nutrition, and the increased population, which will continue to increase, is becoming more and more hungry.

Accordingly, the second factor controlling natural populations is food. The effect of better nutrition is considerable—not only does it give better resistance to disease, a longer life, and better ability to work, but more babies are born and infant mortality is reduced. Adequate nutrition, therefore, means a further increase in the population. Nevertheless, the already dull and monotonous diet of about two-thirds of mankind will soon verge on actual malnutrition, or even starvation, unless we can utilize all our potential food resources.

For example, a single Canadian wheat-farmer can produce enough wheat in a year to provide a subsistence diet for 800 persons. He uses wide tracts of good land and elaborate machinery. One able-bodied man in the tropics, on the other hand, with simple tools, can produce only enough for six persons. If he can use draught animals he can produce, say, 50 per cent more, while if, with better fertilizers and better tools, he can double his output, he can feed six to twelve persons and release them for occupations other than food production.

It is estimated that if all the land known to be suitable for farming were cultivated with techniques and skills known at present, the world could produce food for ten to twenty-five times the present population. There is, of course, little hope of this happening although we may expect food production by the end of the century to be not only of better quality but also to be about three times as great as at present.

The most important duty of any impoverished country is to feed its nationals adequately, preferably on home-grown food rather than on food bought from the countries already over-wealthy as the result of exported "cash" crops. Agriculture is its most fundamental problem.

The first requirement of agriculture is water. There are vast tracts of land, including much of the Sahara Desert, which, once fertile, now are useless. Some of these tracts could be reclaimed, particularly if fresh water were available, and so a first step must be land planning.

After water, comes the need for the chemicals necessary for plant growth. These may be inorganic salts or complex organic mixtures. Modern scientific methods of refertilizing poor lands can be instituted. One of the great problems affecting the whole world is the disposal of organic waste, much of which, properly processed, could and should be used as fertilizer.

After reconditioning, the land must be used wisely to produce the essentials for a proper diet. Thus, in the tropics, good sugar-cane land will produce about 100 tons of sugar per acre while good wheat or rice land will produce less than half this amount of wheat or rice. But sugar is pure carbohydrate, whereas the cereals have a high protein content —and protein is essential for growth, development, and survival. It is accepted that an adequate diet should contain about 15 per cent protein. It must be remembered that the common starchy foods contain some 10 per cent. Part of the remaining 5 per cent could be obtained from a variety of other sources—for example, from new varieties of green plants suitable for tropical cultivation. Actually, in many undernourished countries the required amount—some twenty million tons—is produced annually even now as a byproduct from the extraction of oil from the high protein seeds grown there; the oil is exported, however, and most of the residue is used to feed animals or make fertilizer or may even be wasted.

The best kind of usable protein is of animal origin and it is generally agreed that there must be some animal protein in the diet. In an impoverished country, the conversion of vegetable protein into animal protein by feeding cattle, sheep, and pigs in the conventional manner is not economical. There is, however, no reason at all why attempts should not be made to exploit lands unsuitable for human food crops by domesticating new species of ruminants. There are several in Africa already almost domesticated, such as the eland, which can become fat on desert lands on which cattle would starve. As a ruminant is a bacterial factory in which micro-organisms convert into protein and fats what to us would be unusable materials, it can utilize lands unsuitable for the production of food crops, or even synthetic materials unsuitable for human nutrition.

There are other sources of protein also very inadequately exploited.

The world consumption of fish, for example, is estimated to be about one-fiftieth part of man's diet, that is, about one gram of fish protein per head; this is less than one-ten thousandth part of the annual produce of the sea. We have made no essential changes in our methods of fishing in the last 500 centuries. Fish production could be increased by bringing the fertilizing salts from the deeps to the surface to supply the raw material for photosynthesis and the production of the plankton which ultimately forms the food of fish. This is what actually happens in the great Humboldt Current off western South America where the deep currents from the Pacific rise against the precipitous continental shelf to mix their minerals with the surface waters, making them the richest fishing grounds in the world. It is well within the bounds of possibility to do this artificially, provided, of course, that the disposers of radioactive wastes do not continue their present irresponsible action of dumping ten million gallons of atomic waste into the sea each year, making fish lethal to eat.

Healthy animals and crops, free from disease, would greatly increase the value of even our existing agriculture. Much of our attention in the past has been concerned with those diseases and parasites which affect man. More recently, we have started to investigate the more acute epizootics affecting animals and, still more recently, the diseases and pests of food plants. We are even now in a position to control and probably eradicate the acute infections in animals, but we have done virtually nothing about the chronic ones which year in and year out rob us of millions of tons of high-grade protein. Pests and diseases in our plants cause an even larger and more important loss of foodstuffs, a loss which cannot be estimated accurately but may well be between one-tenth and one-sixth of all the crops harvested—enough to feed about 300 million people.

Having planned how to improve the land and increase its yield, the next step is to work it, by inducing men to become farmers. In an industrial country in which most people live away from the land in towns and cities, this can be done by offering such material inducements as money and machinery. The problem in a non-industrialized country, or one which is in the process of so developing, is quite a different one. Either the farmer serves a very small community or he is tied to the land to serve the larger communities which are in the process of being urbanized.

Farming is not always regarded as a very desirable occupation but it is undoubtedly the one fundamental trade of mankind. More efficient farming is the base on which any under-developed country must build its future. But unless and until the community is able to provide the farmers with the necessary inducement, compulsion from inside or help from outside in the form of foodstuffs and capital to enable the community to become a producer, are necessary.

No one has yet given much thought to tropical urbanization and it undoubtedly requires a great deal of thought. Nor has the question of how to industrialize the warm countries been considered. Certainly what we consider industrialization in the north is quite unsuitable. Indeed, it is a moot question if these tropical countries should be industrialized. Why, for example, should the tropical native wish to become a factory worker and, in spite of the climate, be made to suffer a western civilization? What right have we, in our ignorance, to attempt to mould him in our own image? Why should he wish to undertake our kind of work—even for himself?

The whole tendency in our western civilization is to decrease the time spent at work and to increase leisure. In the tropics, the native has plenty of leisure even now. In the temperate zone with its cold winter we must work—or put machines to work—to provide shelter, heat, and clothing. In the tropics none of these are essential and food can be picked from the trees. Why should we make tropical man work in our manner against his own inclination?

The population increase is a world problem only in that, in some way or other, it affects all countries, socially, politically, or economically. Each country thinks essentially in terms of its own nationals, no matter how high its moral outlook and, in consequence, each country has a different series of problems.

In North America, we entered a virtually empty continent which had been swept clean by the Pleistocene ice and rendered fertile by its action. We borrowed extensively—our plants and animals from the Old World and from South America, the ideas on which we built our modern culture from the other civilizations, and our populations from all the countries of the earth. It is obvious that a time of accounting for this debt is near at hand and we have to consider how to repay it.

The populations of the western world also are increasing. We still have surpluses of food, but we are running short of water. We can secure water from the sea, however, and have, in fact, already started to do so, and we can secure power from the sea, the sun, or the atom. We have eliminated most infectious diseases and soon will eliminate the others, but we are still far from eliminating or even understanding those non-infectious endogenous diseases which are becoming increasingly common. We cannot eliminate death or the degenerative diseases of old age, but we can probably lengthen the average life span. Accordingly, for a long time to come, we shall have more and more people of a mature age, well fed, and free from nutritional worries.

Some of our resources are still adequate but we are running short of minerals. It might be well to stop and think what *are* resources. Quite obviously they must be living things or sources of power which can be renewed. In the true sense—and the distinction, although not often made, is of fundamental importance—they do not include minerals or fossil fuels or even sources of atomic energy. These cannot be renewed and some day will be exhausted. True resources constitute income, whereas minerals constitute capital.

We are rapidly depleting our *own* resources, often without attempting to replace them for the future. Worse still, we are wasting our *own* assets at an appallingly rapid rate, and we cannot replace them at all—at best we can only substitute. In the last fifty years more minerals have been consumed than throughout the whole previous history of mankind. While this is true of both metallic and non-metallic minerals, the situation is particularly critical with respect to the metals which are even now approaching the point of exhaustion. If we continue our present waste of copper, lead, tin, and zinc, for example, we may expect the available supply to be exhausted by the end of this century; iron will last until well on in the next century and then it too will become scarce. These figures are optimistic and assume no great increase in consumption outside of our western culture; if the under-developed lands increase their industrial demands, the time of exhaustion will be even sooner unless new supplies are found much deeper in the earth or taken from the sea. Conservation of metals is a matter of supreme importance to the world, and especially to North America which annually consumes over three times as great a quantity of these metals as the rest of the world combined—many of the ores being obtained from the under-developed countries.

Our present sources of power, other than wind and water, are the so-called fossil fuels, coal, petroleum, natural gas, and these also are being rapidly exhausted. We are using the reserves of these, large as they are, at an increasingly alarming rate and we are consuming not only our own reserves but also those of the backward peoples.

Our western culture, the organized behaviour of our society, has evolved in a biologically unnatural environment, one in which man can live in places and under circumstances which otherwise would be impossible. Consequently, during the evolution of this culture, our efforts have been focused on the improvement of our material environment, and our technology has developed at a progressively increasing rate, probably faster than the multiplication of our populations. But it is also depleting our natural resources and has virtually destroyed our assets. Conservation is already an urgent necessity for both resources and assets. Even more important is the need for planning ahead. Our technology has stampeded our civilization and, like a runaway horse, must be restrained if that civilization is to survive.

Our problems and our responsibilities, however, are by no means confined to our own way of life. We are inevitably concerned with the problems of the under-developed and underfed peoples of the world because we in large part have, directly or indirectly, produced these problems by our ethics, our commerce, our preventive medicine, and our technology. It is the northern peoples who have attempted to replace Natural Selection by Artificial Selection but who have, without thought for the consequences, failed to provide for an adequate system of control. We have made no attempt to improve on Nature's methods of balancing the populations.

There is no panacea for the problems resulting from these increasing numbers. To assume that our method of life, our type of industrialization, our economy of waste, can be applied as they exist to the needy parts of the world, is simply wishful thinking. However, there are many ways of exploiting existing knowledge which we have not yet attempted to apply to the existing situation.

The first step towards solving these problems is the cultivation of a sense of geography and anthropology. The problems are essentially those affecting man as a social animal in a specific environment of soil and climate and with habits resulting from centuries of living with disease and malnutrition.

The second step is increased and intensive research in the fundamentals of agriculture and animal husbandry; basic research is more easily inaugurated, at least, in a temperate climate. Infinitely more important than any of our much publicized scientific efforts, is the problem of producing more food—food of a type suitable for growing and use in the specific areas of the world where it is most needed. We have done comparatively little to use our tropical forests or our northern wastes for food production. Agriculture is applied photosynthesis, the ability of plants to utilize the energy of sunlight, and probably the most important avenue of research today is to discover the secret of this process. Other applications of the permanent forms of energy to man's livelihood in this world, the adequate harvesting of the sea and the supply of fresh water, obviously also have high priority.

The third step is the application of our existing knowledge to those needy parts of the world to enable their people to develop their own resources and to use them for their own advantage rather than ours. This will involve training these people at a level which will be understood by the primitive agriculturists. This means education and propaganda of the most basic and most important kind.

Charity is no answer to their problems. Free food is a palliative measure and so are renewed public health efforts. Steps must be taken *locally* to make the people self-supporting. Immigration is no answer either; the population will continue to increase at a rate which will at least neutralize this help. There is no doubt whatever that, for decades to come, we shall have too many people with too little food, most of them with too little help and knowledge to maintain health, and too little control of their own assets and resources.

The only answer is to increase food production locally faster than the population increases. This, it is true, is only an interim measure but it will help the present situation as well as that which will develop for some years to come. More and better food cannot be produced immediately, however, because the necessary techniques must be employed by the countries themselves. Our present considerable knowledge of agricultural and soil sciences, of reasonable nutrition and better personal health can only be applied by the people themselves. It is essential, then, to have instructors who not only understand the local social customs and cultures, but who also can explain simply and convincingly how to improve them. There is still only a very minor place for the high powered scientist in most of these countries and the vital need is for very simple training rather than post-graduate university education. Culture, the result of education, has as its function the making of a life, training that of making a living, and in these underdeveloped countries, training must come first. Low living and high thinking is a product of old established cultures.

This discussion has so far been confined to the immediate future. The solution of these problems is possible, provided we are prepared to undertake the necessary revision of our own way of life, and plan on a world basis. The greater problem still remains—how to balance births and deaths, not only at home but throughout the world as well, and hold them on a level which will correspond to the upper portion of the population curve. As yet, we have no satisfactory answer to this problem. If it is not to be an increase in the proportion of deaths from starvation, disease, or war, it must come by decreasing numbers of births. There are no possible alternatives; unless this is done, sooner or later the world will reach a stage when there are far too many people and such a situation means universal catastrophe.

We are in the third of a series of major population increases. The first followed the discovery of agriculture, the second the advent of industry, the present, the conquest of disease. The first was universal; the second was essentially a feature of western civilization which only now is affecting the rest of the temperate zones. The third, built on the other two, is really only beginning but is universal in its scope. A variety of factors have prevented the first two rises from becoming catastrophic—the most important of these being disease and violent death, nature's most usual cure for too large and unmanageable populations. We can still further reduce disease even if we cannot eliminate it and we can possibly reduce violent death (even though we are killing more people in North America by automobiles than we ever have done by war). In the future, then, the decisive factor in controlling the population of the world will be the extent of our resources, those materials and sources of power which we can renew. These resources are finite and their wise utilization for the whole world will determine the actual maximum level of the total population. We have not yet reached this stage and we shall not for some generations to come, but the time to start constructive thinking about ways and means is now. There is no evidence that human intelligence is increasing, either in quantity or quality, and consequently the thinking process will be slow and lengthy. Accordingly, all the potential intelligence of mankind must be exploited thoroughly and promptly, so that action can be taken to stabilize the population curve before it can begin its final downward trend.

LE PROBLÈME DE LA POPULATION AU CANADA

Pierre Dagenais

« QU'ON LE VEUILLE OU NON, la poussée démographique arrache la nation canadienne à ses amarres. » Ainsi s'exprimait, en 1956, le rapporteur de la Commission royale d'enquête Gordon sur les perspectives économiques du Canada, après avoir constaté l'accélération du rythme d'accroissement de notre population depuis la fin de la deuxième guerre mondiale. On pouvait alors se questionner sur la durée de cette manifestation de vitalité et par suite sur l'amplitude de ses effets dans la vie économique et sociale du pays. Depuis lors, cinq ans se sont écoulés et le comportement de la population ne fait que confirmer l'affirmation du rapporteur en lui conférant une portée encore plus grande.

Au cours des quinze années qui ont précédé la fin des hostilités, i.e., de 1930 à 1945, le taux moyen annuel de l'accroissement naturel de la population canadienne se fixait à 12 pour-cent (naissances : 21.8 pour-cent; décès : 9.8 pour-cent); depuis la fin de la guerre, i.e., de 1945 à 1960, il s'élève à près de 20 pour-cent (naissances : 27.9 pour-cent; décès 8.3 pour-cent). En chiffres absolus, cela signifie que l'excédent annuel moyen des naissances sur les décès qui était de 135.000 durant la période qui précède 1945, est maintenant de 310.000. Le nombre des naissances a donc plus que doublé et la population canadienne s'enrichit désormais au rythme d'environ un nouveau-né par minute.

A cette jeune armée grandissante de nouveaux consommateurs et futurs producteurs viennent s'ajouter les recrues de l'immigration. Ici encore le parallèle est saisissant. Avant la guerre, le résultat net des mouvements migratoires marquait un déficit annuel moyen d'une dizaine de milliers d'habitants. Le Canada fournissait plus d'hommes à l'étranger qu'il n'en recevait. Au contraire, après la guerre, le bilan migratoire est fortement positif. Durant la période décennale de 1945 à 1956 par exemple, l'immigration grossissait la population canadienne de 70.000 nouveaux habitants en moyenne par année.

Tout compte fait, l'ensemble de la population canadienne qui n'avait gagné que 1.726.000 habitants durant les quinze années qui ont précédé la fin de la guerre (en passant de 10.376.000 en 1930, à 12.107.000 en 1945), s'est grossie de plus de 6 millions d'inhabitants durant les quinze années suivantes (12.102.000 en 1945, 18.145.000 en 1960). Cette montée en flèche de la croissance démographique des années d'après-guerre entraîne des répercussions d'une extrême importance dans la structure économique et sociale du pays.

Cette vigoureuse poussée de la natalité et de l'immigration des quinze dernières années, après l'accalmie de la période précédente, se manifeste déjà sans doute par une considérable augmentation de la population, mais elle ne fait pourtant que commencer en somme à produire ses effets. Elle ne porte encore que sur des éléments jeunes de moins de quinze; les nouveaux besoins qu'elle commence à provoquer sur l'équipement scolaire s'étendront rapidement dans le domaine de l'enseignement secondaire et collégial. Il est à prévoir que la première crête de cette vague démographique atteindra l'université et grossira les rangs de la population dite active vers 1965. Cela signifie pour les années qui viennent une recrudescence inusitée de la nuptialité, des besoins de logements et de produits de toutes sortes. De plus, cette vague qui n'aura jusqu'alors que contribué à l'expansion économique en augmentant le nombre des consommateurs devra, à son tour, passer dans la catégorie des travailleurs. Elle requerra alors des centaines de milliers de nouveaux emplois de plus chaque année.

Le problème de la génération d'après-guerre n'est pas un mythe. Il se posera inéluctablement sous des formes multiples dès que les vagues successives de la présente poussée démographiques commenceront à déferler sur le marché du travail. C'est là un élément avec lequel il faut compter dans la préparation de l'avenir.

Conscient de l'importance de ce phénomène humain, nous nous sommes efforcés d'en évaluer la portée au cours des vingt prochaines années sur la population de la province de Québec. Nous avons ainsi, grâce à la collaboration de plusieurs collègues, géographes et démographes[1], sous les auspices du Ministère provincial de l'Industrie et du Commerce, établi des prévisions d'accroissement naturel par district de recensement, par groupe d'âge quinquennal et par sexe, pour les années 1961, 1966, 1971, 1976 et 1981. Les résultats obtenus ont ensuite été regroupés en fonction des régions économiques de la province.

Ces prévisions ne tiennent aucun compte des mouvements migratoires

[1]MM. Jacques Girard, Michel Bérard, Marcel Bélanger et Jacques Henripin.

pratiquement impossibles à prévoir à l'échelle des districts de recensement; elles contiennent de plus une part plus ou moins grande d'arbitraire dans le choix des taux de mortalité et surtout natalité et de survie. Nous nous permettons de croire cependant qu'elles fournissent une base de spéculation et peut-être même quelques indications utiles aux chercheurs, économistes, politiques, sociologues, démographes ou autres dans les projets d'aménagement territorial et les travaux de planification régionale.

Ces prévisions démographiques, qui donneront bientôt la mesure de leur exactitude à la lumière des résultats du recensement décennal, commencé il y a quelques jours, n'ont guère encore été utilisées, sauf dans le récent ouvrage de M. Michel Phlipponneau sur l' «Avenir économique et social des Cantons de l'Est ».

En attendant le jour où il nous sera possible de les exploiter à fond, nous nous contenterons pour le moment de n'en tirer que quelques commentaires fondamentaux de nature à préciser à l'échelle provinciale les observations que nous appliquions plus haut à l'ensemble du Canada.

L'extraordinaire opposition du comportement démographique entre la période d'avant 1945 et la période d'après-guerre se manifeste ici encore d'une façon étonnante. Durant les quinze années qui ont précédé la fin des hostilités, l'accroissement annuel moyen de la population du Québec était de l'ordre de 45.000; depuis la guerre, il s'élève à plus de 100.000 et il est à prévoir qu'il se fixera à près de 140.000 au cours des quinze années à venir sans tenir compte des possibilités de l'immigration.

La population d'âge scolaire (de cinq à quatorze ans) qui était d'environ 500.000 en 1951, dépasse aujourd'hui le million et atteindra près de 1.800.000 en 1981. Comme la fréquentation scolaire est obligatoire au moins jusqu'à l'âge de quinze ans et que, d'autre part, cette prévision ne tient aucun compte de l'apport éventuel de l'immigration, il nous semble donc que ce soit là un chiffre minimum sur lequel il faille tabler. Cela signifie qu'il sera nécessaire de doubler l'équipement scolaire actuel d'ici quinze ans et qu'il faut prévoir dès maintenant les formidables investissements que représente dans un avenir immédiat la satisfaction d'un des besoins les plus élémentaires de la population.

Une partie plus ou moins grande de cette armée envahissante d'écoliers aspirera à une formation intellectuelle plus poussée. Les spéculations concernant la fréquentation des collèges et des universités sont beaucoup plus délicates à établir que celle des écoles parce qu'elles comportent des éléments variables et des impondérables. Les supputations les plus conservatrices estimaient, en 1956, que le nombre des inscriptions auront doublées vers 1965 lorsque la crête de la première vague démographiques des écoliers actuels atteindra l'âge universitaire.

Cette prévision s'appliquait à l'ensemble du pays. L'augmentation de la gente universitaire se produira sans doute à des rythmes différents d'une province à l'autre. Dans le Québec, pour des raisons d'ordre pédagogique (coordination de l'enseignement) et pécuniaire (gratuité éventuelle), il est permis de croire que l'université deviendra, dans un avenir prochain, plus facilement accessible à l'ensemble de la population qu'elle ne l'a jamais été dans le passé. Il faut donc ajouter ici l'important facteur « accessibilité » à celui de la pression démographique. Cela peut vraisemblablement se traduire par un accroissement du nombre des étudiants proportionnellement plus spectaculaire encore que celui des autres provinces. La population étudiante peut facilement tripler et même quadrupler d'ici quelques dix ou quinze ans. On se rend compte encore une fois de l'importance des investissements nouveaux que ce progrès nous réserve et on peut se demander, en passant, à quelle astuce les gouvernants auront recours pour trouver les fabuleuses sommes d'argent qu'il requiert. S'il est vrai que gouverner c'est prévoir, il ne fait aucun doute que les planificateurs responsables de l'avenir de la province ont du pain sur la planche.

Mais ce n'est peut-être pas encore là le principal problème que suscite l'explosion démographique de l'après-guerre. Considérons maintenant l'évolution de la population active qui est de beaucoup la plus nombreuse sinon la plus importante.

L'université ne retient et ne retiendra malgré tout qu'une faible proportion de la jeunesse. La grande majorité des jeunes achèvent la phase de la préparation à la vie et entrent dans la catégorie des gagne-pain dès la fin des études primaires. C'est pourquoi il est convenu d'inclure dans ce qu'on appelle la population active les groupes de quinze à soixante-quatre ans. Là se recrutent les travailleurs mais hélas aussi les chômeurs de la nation.

Occupons-nous d'abord des recrues de cette armée des travailleurs, c'est-à-dire du groupe des jeunes de quinze à vingt-quatre ans, qui arrivent chaque année dans la société avec un petit bagage d'instruction et un droit indéniable à gagner sa vie honourablement. Le nombre de ces nouveaux venus sur le marché du travail était de l'ordre de 2.300 par année de 1941 à 1951. Il ne présentait aucun problème au cours de cette période d'activité économique exceptionnelle. Mais attention, il sera de 30.000 par année au cours de la prochaine décennie, c'est-à-dire quinze fois plus considérable, abstraction faite de tout mouvement d'immigration possible. L'expansion économique de la période 1961–

71 sera-t-elle proportionnelle à la poussée démographique ? Y aura-t-il un emploi pour tous les nouveaux venus qui en désirent, compte tenu du fait que ce groupe de jeunes représentera une armée de plus de 1.140.000 en 1971, et que la population active totale s'élèvera à plus de 3.700.00 ?

Sans doute, tout le monde de quinze à soixante-quatre ans n'occupe pas un emploi rémunéré. Il y a les incapables, physiques ou mentaux, ils posent des problèmes d'un autre order. Il y a aussi et surtout le contingent de l'élément féminin qui, d'après des barèmes officiels (probablement établis par des hommes) sont classés comme n'ayant pas à gagner leur vie. Ce contingent, autrefois presque universel, tend à diminuer comme chacun sait. Le nombre des femmes du Québec exerçant une fonction rémunérée (officiellement) a passé de 14.7 pour-cent en 1901 à 24.4 pour-cent en 1951 et il ne fait aucun doute que cette proportion sera sensiblement plus forte en 1961 et continuera d'augmenter dans les années à venir. D'autre part le taux masculin d'activité se maintient à plus de 80 pour-cent.

Au total, même en ne tenant aucun compte de l'augmentation probable du taux de l'activité féminine et des apports possibles de l'immigration, on constate que l'accroissement annuel des nouveaux venus sur le marché du travail se fera à un rythme accéléré particulièrement à partir de 1966. On estime alors que les recrues de l'armée des travailleurs pour l'ensemble de la population dite active se totaliseront à plus de 40.000 en 1966, à 45.000 en 1971 et à près de 52.000 en 1981.

La période de surexcitation industrielle et de prospérité économique dès années 1941 à 1951, qui se caractérise par un embauchage exceptionnellement élevé a réussi à absorber une moyenne d'environ 24.000 nouveaux travailleurs par année, hommes et femmes. Cet âge d'or de l'embauchage s'est passablement atténué depuis lors, comme chacun sait. Les statistiques du chômage actuel sont là pour nous le faire constater. Doit-on s'attendre à ce que cet âge d'or revienne au cours des vingt prochaines années et qu'il ait alors doublé ses capacités d'embauchage ? Doit-on au contraire prévoir l'établissement d'une armée grandissante du chômage chronique que seule une transformation profonde de la structure économique ne parviendrait à atténuer ?

Pendant que la population active se développera dans les proportions que nous venons d'évoquer, le fardeau des vieillards dans la société deviendra de son côté de plus en plus lourd à supporter. Les Québécois qui avaient atteint l'âge de la retraite, c'est-à-dire soixante-cinq ans, étaient au nombre de 230.000 en 1951; ils seront 300.000 de plus en 1981. Leur nombre augmentera ainsi en moyenne d'une dizaine de milliers chaque année. En marge des institutions qui disposent déjà d'un fond de pension, la structure sociale et l'équipement hospitalier actuels suffiront-ils à la tâche ? Dans quelle mesure doit-on prévoir le développement des hospices et des maisons de retraite ?

Voilà quelques questions, entre bien d'autres, qui se posent à l'esprit lorsqu'on s'arrête un instant à considérer les effets de l'étonnante poussée démographique de l'après-guerre.

LA MAIN-D'ŒUVRE CANADIENNE

Guy Rocher

JE ME PROPOSE, dans le cadre de ces exposés, d'aborder un aspect bien délimité de l'évolution de la population canadienne, à savoir celui de l'évolution de la population au travail. Ce n'est là qu'une partie de l'ensemble du tableau que présente l'histoire de la population canadienne, mais c'est une partie qui concerne une portion assez importante de la population, c'est-à-dire au moins la moitié. Au surplus, nous verrons qu'à partir de l'analyse de la population au travail se posent des questions fondamentales sur l'évolution de l'ensemble de notre société canadienne.

Lorsqu'on parle de population au travail, on entend depuis quelques années une catégorie très précise de la population que l'on appelle la main-d'œuvre. Cette dernière notion, très courante aujourd'hui, est pourtant récente, du moins avec la précision que nous lui connaissons maintenant. C'est en particulier à l'occasion de la crise économique des années trente qu'on se rendit compte, tant dans les pays européens qu'aux Etats-Unis, de l'imprécision des notions utilisées jusqu'alors pour désigner la population qui travaille, et pour distinguer ceux qui ont un emploi de ceux qui n'en ont pas. En particulier, lorsque les gouvernements voulurent connaître l'étendue du chômage qui accompagnait la crise économique, on dut se rendre compte — même si cela peut nous étonner aujourd'hui — que l'on n'avait pas une définition assez précise du chômage pour mesurer ce phénomène avec exactitude. Distinguer entre les travailleurs en emploi et ceux qui sont sans emploi pour l'ensemble d'une population constitue en effet un problème technique beaucoup plus complexe qu'il n'apparaît à première vue. Il fallut plusieurs années d'étude et d'expérimentation, et la coordination des efforts des statisticiens du travail pour développer une technique de mesure valable, basée sur des distinctions satisfaisantes.

Or, ce sont ces recherches sur le chômage qui ont amené à préciser du même coup la notion de main-d'œuvre que nous connaissons aujourd'hui. Car on s'aperçut que ce n'est qu'en considérant le chômage dans la main-d'œuvre et par rapport à la main-d'œuvre que l'on peut en dégager une notion précise et mensurable. Le chômage est donc devenu une sous-catégorie de la main-d'œuvre. C'est ainsi que le Bureau Fédéral de la Statistique, dans ses rapports mensuels sur l'état de la main-d'œuvre, définit celle-ci de la façon suivante : « La main-d'œuvre civile se compose de la partie de la population civile âgée de 14 ans et plus et qui, durant la semaine du relevé, était employée ou en chômage. » Sans entrer dans le détail des distinctions qu'appelle cette définition, la main-œuvre comprend à la fois les « employés » et les « chômeurs ». Les employés sont tous ceux qui ont travaillé, durant une période déterminée, ne fût-ce que quelques heures, dans un emploi reconnu soit pour un employeur ou pour leur propre compte et qui en ont retiré une rémunération ou un bénéfice ou qui ont contribué sans rémunération à une entreprise familiale. Par contre, le chômeur est celui qui, durant la période considérée, ne travaillait pas et cherchait activement un emploi ou en aurait normalement cherché un, ou encore qui était en congédiement temporaire pour une période de moins de trente jours. Le chômeur, ainsi défini, appartient à la main-d'œuvre parce qu'il fait partie du capital humain disponible pour le travail productif de la nation. Par contre, les étudiants et les mères de famille ne font pas partie de ce capital humain économiquement productif, quelles que soient leurs heures de travail; ils font partie de la population non-active, avec les malades chroniques, les inactifs volontaires, les retraités et les prisonniers.

Ainsi définie par le Bureau Fédéral de la Statistique, la main-d'œuvre représente en 1961 53 pour-cent de l'ensemble de la population de quatorze ans et plus. C'est sur cette moitié de la population canadienne que vont porter les remarques qui suivent. Il n'est évidemment pas possible, dans l'espace alloué, de considérer l'évolution de notre main-d'œuvre dans toutes ses dimensions. Nous n'en considérerons que certaines caractéristiques qui nous paraissent plus particulièrement significatives. Nous analyserons d'abord l'évolution de la main-d'œuvre globale depuis le début de ce siècle, pour considérer ensuite l'évolution de certains secteurs de la main-d'œuvre, tels que la main-d'œuvre âgée, la main-d'œuvre féminine et la main-d'œuvre en chômage.

Pour faire d'abord l'analyse de l'évolution de la main-d'œuvre globale, la classification de la main-d'œuvre la plus simple et la plus significative est celle qui partage les occupations en trois grands secteurs : les secteurs primaire, secondaire et tertiaire. Le secteur primaire comprend les occupations dont les travailleurs sont en contact direct avec les richesses naturelles : agriculture, mines, pêche, abattage du bois. Le secteur secondaire recouvre les occupations dont le travail consiste à fabriquer ou construire, ce qui comprend tout travail d'usine et tous les emplois de construction. Le secteur tertiaire est constitué des emplois qui concernent la distribution des biens (commerce, transport, finance) et tous les emplois non-manuels (travail de bureau, travail professionnel, services).

Si l'on classifie la main-d'œuvre canadienne selon ces trois secteurs, on observe une transformation radicale dans les cinquante dernières années. En 1901, 51 pour-cent de la main-d'œuvre canadienne était employée dans les occupations primaires, alors qu'il n'en reste plus que 26 pour-cent en 1951 et cette proportion est sûrement encore plus faible en 1961. En d'autres termes, on ne trouve plus qu'une personne sur quatre dans ce secteur, au lieu d'une personne sur deux en 1901. Ce sont les occupations tertiaires (services, commerce, professions) qui ont bénéficié de la contraction du secteur primaire. Elles ont en effet passé de 27 pour-cent en 1901 à 48 pour-cent en 1951. Les occupations secondaires de leur côté sont demeurées proportionnellement assez stables, évoluant entre 18 et 25 pour-cent[1].

Ces chiffres résument en quelque sorte la période de rapide industrialisation qu'a connu notre pays dans les dernières décennies. En 1901, la structure économique et sociale de notre pays était fortement appuyée sur l'agriculture et le monde rural : 40 pour-cent de la main-d'œuvre était alors employée dans l'agriculture. Il n'en restait plus que 18 pour-cent en 1951 et 10 pour-cent en 1960. Cette évolution est encore plus frappante si l'on observe que les agriculteurs ont diminué non seulement proportionnellement mais aussi en nombre absolu. Depuis au moins quinze ans, leur nombre a décru de façon constante, passant de 1.186.000 en 1946 à 675.000 en 1960[2]. L'agriculture, qui jouait encore un rôle dominant au début de ce siècle n'occupe plus qu'une très faible minorité de notre main-d'œuvre.

Par contre, le nombre de personnes employées dans les usines et manufactures a triplé en cinquante ans, les emplois de commerce et de finance se sont multipliés par cinq, ceux des transports par six, et ceux des bureaux par dix.

Cette évolution n'est évidemment pas propre au Canada. Elle a été observée par l'économiste anglais Colin Clark et l'économiste français Jean Fourastié pour tous les pays industrialisés ou en voie d'industrialisation[3]. Cependant, les comparaisons établies entre les pays par ces

[1]Patrick Allen, « Tendances récentes des occupations au Canada » , *L'Actualité économique* (avril-juin, 1956).
[2]*La Main-d'œuvre* (Bureau Fédéral de la Statistique, avril, 1961), Tableaux 1 et 2.
[3]Colin Clark, *The Conditions of Economic Progress* (New York : St. Martin's Press, Inc., 1957), et Jean Fourastié, *La Civilisation de 1975*.

chercheurs nous permettent d'affirmer que le Canada, par suite du rapide dégonflement de son secteur primaire et de l'accroissement parallèle du secteur tertiaire, est devenu en peu de temps un des pays les plus hautement industrialisés du monde.

Il faut cependant ajouter que le processus que nous venons de décrire s'applique à l'ensemble de la main-d'œuvre canadienne. Il ne se produit cependant pas au même rythme dans toutes les régions de notre pays. Cette évolution s'est produite à un rythme très rapide dans l'Ontario, le Québec et la Colombie Britannique, et à un tempo plus lent dans les autres provinces, en particulier l'Ile du Prince Edouard, le Nouveau Brunswick et la Saskatchewan.

Cette brève description de l'évolution qu'a connu l'ensemble de la main-d'œuvre canadienne nous permettra maintenant de mieux comprendre les changements qui se sont produits dans certaines catégories plus spécifiques de travailleurs. La première de ces catégories que je veux considérer est celle des travailleurs âgés, c'est-à-dire de soixante-cinq ans et plus. On observe très peu de femmes de cette catégorie dans la main-d'œuvre. Mais on note chez les hommes de cette catégorie une tendance très marquée à se retirer de la main-d'œuvre. Cette tendance a été constante depuis plusieurs années. Ainsi en 1945, 50 pour-cent des hommes de soixante-cinq ans et plus étaient encore en emploi; en 1958, cette proportion était tombée à 32 pour-cent[4]. Il ne semble pas encore se dessiner de mouvement de retraite marqué chez les travailleurs de soixante à soixante-cinq ans. Cette tendance à la retraite après soixante-cinq ans est évidemment le résultat, pour une large part, du développement des divers plans de pension adoptés par les entreprises et la généralisation des allocations de sécurité sociale aux personnes âgées. Elle indique cependant aussi l'apparition de nouvelles attitudes, de nouvelles normes de comportement de notre population âgée à l'endroit de la retraite, qui se généralise de plus en plus. Nous pouvons tirer de là deux observations assez importantes. La première est que notre société devra se préoccuper de plus en plus des problèmes liés à la retraite et aux « vieux jours », car ces problèmes risquent de devenir aigus dans notre civilisation urbaine : problèmes de logements, d'institutions, de loisirs, etc. En second lieu, nous observons un raccourcissement très net de ce que l'on peut appeler « la vie de travail » . En effet, non seulement les hommes âgés de soixante-cinq ans et plus se retirent de la main-d'œuvre, mais les jeunes hommes de moins de vingt ans y entrent en moins grand nombre. Alors que de cinquante-cinq à 60 pour-cent des jeunes hommes de quatorze à dix-neuf ans faisaient partie de la main-d'œuvre en 1945,

---

[4]*La Main-d'œuvre*, Document de référence no. 58, revision de 1958 (Bureau Fédéral de la Statistique, novembre, 1945 — juillet, 1958), pp. 52–3.

on n'en trouve que de quarante à 50 pour-cent en 1958[5]. On peut donc dire que la période active du Canadien se réduit par les deux extrémités. C'est en conséquence de plus en plus exclusivement sur la population de vingt à soixante-cinq ans que repose la responsabilité de l'activité productive de la nation.

La seconde catégorie de travailleurs dont l'évolution a été très caractéristique, est celle des femmes. Le nombre de femmes dans la main-d'œuvre, en chiffres absolus et proportionnellement, s'est accru de façon constante depuis le début du siècle. A ce moment, environ une femme sur dix travaillait, et c'était généralement pour des raisons économiques impérieuses. En 1961, 28 pour-cent des femmes canadiennes de quatorze ans et plus sont inscrites dans la main-d'œuvre, particulièrement dans les emplois tertiaires (bureau, commerce, services). Cette proportion continue à s'accroître en dépit des périodes de chômage que nous connaissons; il est d'ailleurs remarquable que le taux de chômage des femmes est extrêmement bas, en partie parce que les femmes — surtout les femmes mariées — se retirent de la main-d'œuvre lorsqu'elles tombent en chômage, mais surtout, à mon avis, parce que les industries et surtout les occupations qui les attirent n'ont pas souffert des périodes de récession.

La distribution de la main-d'œuvre féminine par groupes d'âge est importante à analyser. On sait tout d'abord que ce sont surtout les jeunes femmes qui sont attirées par le marché du travail; une moyenne de 45 pour-cent à 50 pour-cent des femmes de vingt à vingt-quatre ans travaillent, soit environ une sur deux. Cette moyenne s'est maintenue de façon très stable depuis 1945. Par contre les jeunes femmes de moins de vingt ans ont marqué une légère tendance à la baisse, passant d'une moyenne d'environ 37 pour-cent en 1945 à une moyenne d'environ 30 pour-cent en 1960. Il est cependant très remarquable que les femmes de quarante-cinq à soixante-quatre ans ont été de plus en plus attirées par le marché du travail dans les dernières années; 15 pour-cent d'entr'elles étaient en emploi en 1945 alors qu'il y en avait 28 pour-cent en 1960. Cette tendance semble indiquer un mouvement de retour au travail chez la femme mariée dont les enfants sont assez âgés pour ne plus requérir les soins maternels constants. Un tel mouvement a été très marqué aux Etats-Unis et il paraît se manifester aussi chez nous de façon de plus en plus nette.

Il s'accompagne d'ailleurs effectivement d'une augmentation croissante de la représentation des femmes mariées dans la main-d'œuvre. En 1945, 30 pour-cent des femmes en emploi étaient mariées, sans

[5]*Ibid.*

compter les veuves, divorcées et séparées; en 1960, cette proportion s'élevait en 43 pour-cent, soit près de la moitié.

Nous pouvons donc dire que nous assistons à une profonde modification du statut de la femme, qui implique plus profondément l'apparition de ce que l'on pourrait appeler une nouvelle « philosophie de la femme ». La femme n'est plus perçue comme étant seulement la mère ou l'éducatrice. Elle a aussi une part de plus en plus grande à l'activité économique de la nation. On l'invite à accepter de nouvelles tâches en dehors du foyer; certaines occupations de bureau ou de commerce lui sont presque exclusivement réservées (téléphoniste, secrétaire, dactylo). C'est là une évolution psycho-sociologique qui marquera très profondément notre société de l'avenir et qui méritera d'être étudiée de très près.

Pour terminer ces remarques, disons quelques mots d'une troisième catégorie de la main-d'œuvre, celle qui est en chômage. Nous avons vu plus haut que les chômeurs constituent un réservoir de capital humain productif et sont comptés à ce titre dans la main-d'œuvre. On parle beaucoup du chômage depuis quelque temps. Et selon tout apparence il faudra en parler encore pendant assez longtemps, car les prévisions des économistes sont loin d'être optimistes. Nous n'avons rien à ajouter à ce sujet. Nous voulons seulement indiquer que le chômage touche tout particulièrement deux groupes de travailleurs. Ce sont d'abord les jeunes travailleurs. En effet, selon les derniers renseignements du Bureau Fédéral de la Statistique pour le premier trimestre de 1961, 25 pour-cent des jeunes hommes de quatorze à dix-neuf ans étaient en chômage et 19 pour-cent des jeunes travailleurs de vingt à vingt-quatre ans, alors que la moyenne de chômage des hommes s'établissait à 13 pour-cent pour la même période[6]. C'est donc dire que les jeunes travailleurs, surtout ceux de moins de vingt ans, ont beaucoup de difficulté à entrer sur le marché du travail. Il est donc heureux que, comme nous l'avons vu tout à l'heure, les jeunes tendent à entrer plus tard sur le marché du travail, ce qui veut dire qu'ils étendent plus longtemps la période de scolarité, car on sait que les travailleurs les plus touchés par le chômage sont ceux qui ne jouissent pas d'une instruction ou d'une spécialisation suffisante. En effet, le deuxième groupe de chômeurs le plus remarquable est celui des journaliers, manœuvres et ouvriers non spécialisés. Trente-trois pour-cent, soit le tiers de ces travailleurs étaient en chômage durant le premier trimestre de 1961, représentant à eux seuls 20 pour-cent de tous les chômeurs canadiens. Nous n'avons malheureusement pas les renseignements nécessaires pour estimer la proportion de jeunes travailleurs parmi les journaliers et ouvriers non spécialisés; nous pouvons

[6]*La Main-d'œuvre* (Bureau Fédéral de la Statistique, avril, 1961), p. 8.

cependant croire qu'elle est assez élevée car les jeunes de quatorze à dix-neuf ans n'ont guère eu la chance, pour la plupart, d'acquérir une formation technique ou une qualification occupationnelle. Il est donc clair que notre société industrialisée n'a plus que faire des travailleurs qui n'ont pas un minimum d'instruction, de spécialisation ou de qualification. Celui qui pouvait autrefois, avec la seule force de ses bras, trouver quelque travail à faire est aujourd'hui mis de côté par une structure industrielle de plus en plus mécanisée et qui requiert une population de travailleurs plus instruits et plus spécialisés. Nous voyons ici à l'évidence comment il est urgent de repenser à la fois notre système d'enseignement général et spécialisé, en vue de préparer la jeunesse à entrer dans un monde économique qui puisse l'accueillir.

Pour conclure ces trop brèves remarques, nous voulons insister sur le fait que, comme nous croyons l'avoir suggéré, l'analyse de la main-d'œuvre permet de photographier, ou plus exactement de filmer l'évolution d'une société comme la nôtre. Elle étale devant nos yeux le panorama de la marche poursuivie et les principales étapes traversées. Elle permet aussi de poser certains problèmes contemporains liés à cette évolution ou qui en résultent assez directement. Nous avons vu en particulier comment l'analyse de l'évolution de la main-d'œuvre canadienne depuis cinquante ans décrit de façon dramatique la rapide industrialisation et l'urbanisation massive de notre pays, et le mouvement irréversible dans lequel nous sommes engagés. Une nouvelle société s'élabore ainsi devant nos yeux, dans laquelle l'instruction et la spécialisation deviennent essentielles, où les jeunes entreront plus tard sur le marché du travail tandis que les personnes âgées s'en retireront plus tôt, et où la femme, même la femme mariée, est invitée à remplir des fonctions dans la productivité nationale.

Telles sont quelques unes des questions que soulève une rapide analyse de notre population au travail.

ÉVOLUTION DE LA COMPOSITION ETHNIQUE ET LINGUISTIQUE DE LA POPULATION CANADIENNE

Jacques Henripin

LA COMPOSITION ETHNIQUE ET LINGUISTIQUE de la population canadienne est un sujet sérieux et délicat; il s'agit là de caractères qui ont une influence profonde sur le comportement des individus, de même que sur les institutions et, d'autre part, on ne saurait se cacher que la plupart des Canadiens sont assez sensibles aux modifications qui peuvent intervenir dans l'importance relative de chacun de ces groupes ethniques ou linguistiques.

Ces circonstances ne m'ont cependant pas convaincu de m'abstenir de faire certaines perspectives, même si mes calculs sont loin d'être aussi prudents ou raffinés qu'ils pourraient l'être. Et je m'excuse à l'avance du caractère un peu hasardeux de certaines d'entre elles. Je m'attacherai à trois questions : La population canadienne devient-elle plus homogène ou plus hétérogène ? Que représentent la langue anglaise et la langue française comme puissance d'attraction des divers groupes ethniques ou linguistiques ? Enfin, la dualité culturelle du Canada est-elle menacée ou assurée par l'évolution probable de la proportion des Canadiens dont la langue maternelle est le français ?

HOMOGÉNÉITÉ

Si l'on se place au point de vue de l'origine ethnique, il paraît évident que la population canadienne est devenue de moins en moins homogène, au cours des soixante-dix dernières années. D'abord, le groupe ethnique principal (les Britanniques) a perdu de l'importance et il n'a plus la majorité absolue. Les Français, eux, ont à peu près maintenu leur proportion (voisine de 30 pour-cent). Depuis 1921, cette proportion a manifesté une légère tendance à croître. L'ensemble des autres groupes ethniques a doublé son importance et la fraction que ces groupes représentent est passée de 11 pour-cent en 1881 à 22 pour-cent environ en 1951.

Si ces tendances se maintenaient, on trouverait, vers l'an 2000, une population à peu près également partagée en trois groupes : Britanniques, Français et autres origines. Remarquons en passant que, dans une province, la Saskatchewan, les Britanniques et les Français réunis ne formaient plus, en 1951, la majorité absolue et que la situation des deux autres provinces des prairies était voisine de celle-là.

Mais on ne saurait se baser uniquement sur l'origine ethnique pour se faire une idée de l'homogénéité culturelle de la population canadienne. Si l'on fait l'hypothèse que la plus grande partie des traits culturels particuliers disparaissent avec l'adoption d'une langue maternelle qui ne correspond plus à l'origine ethnique, la population canadienne apparaît beaucoup plus homogène et elle le deviendra probablement de plus en plus. Alors que plus de 20 pour-cent des habitants du Canada, en 1951, avaient une origine ethnique qui n'était ni britannique ni française, on n'en trouvait que 12 pour-cent dont la langue maternelle n'était ni l'anglais ni le français. Et, depuis 1931, cette proportion diminue. Elle était encore de 14.4 pour-cent en 1941.

En 1951, environ la moitié des Canadiens qui étaient d'origine non britannique ni française avaient adopté l'une des deux langues officielles du pays comme langue maternelle. Cette proportion avait crû rapidement au cours des années précédentes.

En fait, c'est la langue anglaise qui est adoptée par les Néo-Canadiens et non le français. Si bien que, même si le groupe ethnique britannique voit son importance diminuer, le groupe linguistique anglais, lui, gagne du terrain. Entre 1941 et 1951, la proportion des Canadiens dont la langue maternelle est l'anglais est passée de 56.4 pour-cent à 59.1 pourcent. Le français a perdu un peu de poids, mais cela doit s'expliquer par l'entrée de Terre-Neuve dans les statistiques de 1951.

Cela m'amène à ma deuxième question, c'est-à-dire au rôle du français et de l'anglais comme pôles d'attraction linguistique.

PÔLES D'ATTRACTION LINGUISTIQUE

Il n'y a qu'un pôle d'attraction : c'est l'anglais. Parmi les Canadiens non britanniques ni français qui ont abandonné leur langue d'origine, il n'y a pas plus de 2 ou 3 pour-cent qui ont adopté le français comme langue maternelle. Parmi les groupes ethniques de quelque importance, il n'y en a guère que deux qui atteignent des proportions plus élevées : les Italiens, avec 11 pour-cent et les Indiens, avec 9 pour-cent. Mais même pour ces deux groupes, l'attraction du français est très faible.

On ne peut donc pas parler du français comme pôle d'attraction linguistique, même pas dans la province de Québec. Dans cette province, il n'y a que les Italiens qui adoptent plus facilement le français que l'anglais.

Si le français occupe encore une position majeure, au Canada, c'est à titre de facteur de rétention ou de résistance et non à titre de facteur d'attraction. Il n'arrive tout au plus qu'à retenir ceux qui ont déjà le français comme langue maternelle. Et d'ailleurs, il n'y arrive que bien imparfaitement. Les Canadiens d'origine française ne semblent pas résister beaucoup plus que les autres groupes ethniques à l'attraction de l'anglais.

Il est intéressant, à cet égard, de suivre l'évolution de la proportion des Canadiens français qui adoptent l'anglais comme langue maternelle. On peut la connaître depuis 1921. Or, cette proportion croît suivant une progression à peu près rigoureusement géométrique. Elle était de 3.5 pour-cent en 1921, 7.9 pour-cent en 1951 et si cette progression s'est maintenue, c'est une proportion de 10 pour-cent environ que le recensement de 1961 va révéler.

Evidemment, ces transferts linguistiques n'ont pas la même intensité partout. Ils ne représentaient, en 1951, que 1.5 pour-cent des Français du Québec et 30 pour-cent de ceux qui vivent hors du « glacier québécois ». Le phénomène est donc lié, très étroitement, à ce qu'on pourrait appeler la « densité ethnique » des Canadiens français dans les différentes régions du pays. Il est d'ailleurs intéressant de remarquer qu'à « densité » égale, les Canadiens français adoptent l'anglais deux ou trois fois plus que ne le font les Britanniques pour le français.

Devant de tels faits, on peut se demander si la dualité culturelle n'est pas menacée au Canada. Plus précisément, la question que je pose est la suivante : quelles conjectures peut-on faire sur la fraction de la population canadienne dont la langue maternelle sera le français, d'ici une cinquantaine d'années ?

PROPORTION FUTURE DE LA POPULATION DE LANGUE MATERNELLE FRANÇAISE

On est en présence de trois faits majeurs : (*a*) des Canadiens d'origine non britannique ni française, qui adoptent progressivement, en presque totalité, la langue anglaise; (*b*) des Canadiens d'origine britannique dont l'importance diminue, mais dont les rangs sont grossis, au point de vue linguistique, par les Néo-Canadiens; (*c*) des Canadiens d'origine française, dont la proportion est à peu près stable, mais dont une fraction appréciable abandonne le français pour l'anglais.

Il s'agit donc de se demander quelle pourra être, dans l'avenir, la proportion de la population canadienne dont la langue maternelle restera le français. C'est ici que commencent les calculs hasardeux.

Il faut tenir compte d'au moins trois phénomènes : la croissance naturelle des Canadiens français et des autres Canadiens; l'immigration; et les transferts linguistiques des Canadiens français qui adoptent l'anglais.

Commençons par la croissance naturelle et supposons d'abord qu'il n'y a ni migration ni transfert linguistique. Il n'est pas facile de prédire la croissance naturelle pour une période de cinquante ou soixante ans. Aussi ai-je fait deux hypothèses qui me paraissent assez extrêmes, de sorte que la réalité a passablement de chances de se trouver entre les résultats de ces deux hypothèses. Suivant la première hypothèse, les taux de reproduction respectifs des Français et des non Français, en 1951, se maintiendront jusqu'en 2011. Comme les premiers se reproduisent plus vite, leur proportion augmente : elle serait de 34 pour-cent en 1981 et 37 pour-cent en 2011. Cette hypothèse est évidemment très favorable à la croissance du groupe français, puisqu'elle maintient — contre toute probabilité — l'écart entre les taux de reproduction.

La seconde hypothèse veut que les taux de reproduction s'abaissent progressivement pour atteindre l'unité en 2011. Dans ces conditions, la proportion des Canadiens français passerait à 33.6 pour cent en 1981 et à 34.7 pour-cent en 2011. Ici, il existe encore un écart entre les taux de reproduction, mais cet écart s'amenuise progressivement pour s'annuler en 2011.

Mais l'immigration vient annuler cette croissance de l'importance des Canadiens français. Si l'on suppose une immigration nette de 100,000 personnes par an, la proportion que représentent les Canadiens français devient plus faible que celle qu'on observait en 1951 (31 pour-cent). Pour 1981, on a 28.8 pour-cent avec la première hypothèse et 27.8 pour-cent avec la seconde. Pour 2011, on a 29 pour-cent et 24 pour-cent.

Faisons maintenant intervenir le dernier phénomène : la fraction croissante des Canadiens d'origine française qui adoptent l'anglais. J'ai déjà signalé que cette fraction avait augmenté, entre 1921 et 1951, suivant une progression géométrique. Si cette progression se maintenait, la fraction serait de 18 pour-cent en 1981 et 40 pour-cent en 2011. Avant d'appliquer de telles proportions, il y a lieu de se demander si elles sont vraisemblables. En faisant des calculs séparés pour les Canadiens français du Québec et ceux des autres provinces, on est amené à diminuer quelque peu ces proportions. Finalement, j'ai retenu les proportions suivantes : 15 pour-cent en 1981 et 30 pour-cent en 2011.

Voyons maintenant ce que devient la proportion des Canadiens de langue maternelle française, en tenant compte de la croissance naturelle, de l'immigration et de l'adoption de la langue anglaise par une fraction importante des Canadiens d'origine française.

Dans l'hypothèse du maintien des taux de reproduction de 1951 — qui ne me paraît pas très vraisemblable mais qui présente l'intérêt d'être particulièrement favorable au maintien du groupe de langue française — on obtient, pour 1981, 24.5 pour-cent; et pour 2011, 20 pour-cent. Dans l'autre hypothèse — diminution progressive des taux de reproduction — la proportion de la population canadienne dont la langue maternelle est le français serait de 23.5 pour-cent en 1981 et 17 pour-cent en 2011. Le tableau suivant résume les résultats qu'on obtient lorsqu'on fait intervenir successivement les trois facteurs mentionnés.

PROPORTION FUTURE DES CANADIENS DONT LA LANGUE MATERNELLE EST LE FRANÇAIS, SUIVANT LES PHÉNOMÈNES QU'ON FAIT INTERVENIR (EN POURCENTAGES)

| Hypothèse sur la croissance naturelle | Phenomènes qui interviennent | | | | | |
| | Accroissement naturel seulement | | Accroissement naturel et migrations | | Accroissement naturel, migrations et transferts linguistiques | |
	1981	2011	1981	2011	1981	2011
1. Forte croissance	33.9	37.0	28.8	29.0	24.5	20.3
2. Croissance déclinante	33.6	34.7	27.8	24.1	23.7	16.8

Je ne prétends pas que ces perspectives représentent avec certitude ce qui va se passer dans l'avenir. Elles reposent sur des hypothèses et ne peuvent avoir plus de valeur que ces hypothèses elles-mêmes. Mais il semble difficile d'admettre que la fraction de la population canadienne dont le français est la langue maternelle va se maintenir. Il faudrait pour cela que les immigrants se rallient en grand nombre à la langue française et que les Canadiens français eux-mêmes cessent d'adopter, en proportion croissante, la langue anglaise. On ne voit pas très bien comment le premier phénomène pourrait se produire, ni pourquoi le deuxième phénomène cesserait.

Cela étant, il semble bien que, vers 1980, la proportion des Canadiens d'expression française sera comprise entre 23 et 25 pour-cent et que vers 2010 elle sera comprise entre 16.5 et 20.5 pour-cent. Rappelons que cette proportion était de 29 pour-cent en 1951.

Cela ne signifie pas la disparition du fait français au Canada. Mais la culture française est probablement assez compromise à l'extérieur du Québec, sauf, peut-être, au Nouveau-Brunswick. Dans le Québec, la fraction des Canadiens français qui adoptent l'anglais ne dépassera probablement pas 10 pour-cent en l'an 2011. Et d'ailleurs, ce phénomène a été, jusqu'à maintenant, compensé par ceux des autres origines qui adoptent le français. Mais, dans les autres provinces, la tendance des trente dernières années est inquiétante. Bien entendu, il n'est pas certain qu'elle se poursuivra au même rythme. Si elle le faisait, on assisterait probablement à la disparition de la langue française hors du Québec et du Nouveau Brunswick.

NEW PATTERNS IN THE BIRTH RATE[1]

Nathan Keyfitz, F.R.S.C.

BETWEEN THE 1870's and the 1940's the birth rate showed certain trends and differentials so consistently that these seemed to be a universal law: that progress in any country or region results in steadily diminishing numbers of children, and at any given moment the birth rate must be especially low for the people who are better off, more educated, and more urban than for those who do not have these advantages; the constant prospect for the future was that the remaining poor would have children and the rich would choose to apply their wealth to getting richer. When population problems were discussed in Europe and America, the one which tended to be stressed was whether the low fertility groups, often characterized by the epithet "advanced," would not simply die out.

The 1950's have now shown an unexpected reversal in the trends and differentials which calls for some restatement both of the world and of the Canadian prospect. A new stability has appeared in the relative positions of countries, along with new relations among statistically identifiable groups within countries. Pending the 1961 Census of Canada and recent censuses of other countries, it is not possible to make final assertions on all details; this paper appearing in 1962 may be regarded as in part a "prediction" of what the situation was in 1961. One of the advantages of the new electronic equipment which enables the Dominion Bureau of Statistics to make quick and complete tabulations of the census is that if these predictions are wrong they will be more quickly exposed by the published facts than they could have been with the tabulation methods used in earlier censuses.

We may summarize the international aspect of the new and apparently

[1]The writer would like to acknowledge the valuable assistance of Mr. A. H. LeNeveu of the Dominion Bureau of Statistics. For an analysis of United States data which has directed attention to phenomena similar to those of this paper, see Paul Glick, *American Families* (New York: Wiley, 1957).

stable pattern of the birth rate as a division of the countries of the world into three very distinct categories whose birth rates hardly overlap. The categories may be described in terms of income and available space per person: thus the three groups into which countries fall when classified according to their birth rates are those which are poor, those which are moderately well off, industrialized, and crowded, and those which are well off and have ample space in relation to the number of their people. It is to the emergence of this last group, with its evidently stable birth rate at a level quite different from that of the other two groups, that we wish particularly to call attention.

The members of the first group include most of the countries of Asia except Japan and most of Latin America except the Argentine Republic. They are typified by Mexico with 44.5 births per thousand population in 1958, Peru with 37.6, Ceylon with 36.5. In these countries birth figures are often understated and sometimes lacking altogether; included are both India and China whose level one supposes to be in the neighbourhood of 40 per thousand (the Indian National Sample Survey showed a birth rate of 39 per thousand in rural parts in 1958). Although the lack of data makes it impossible to identify all the countries that belong to this group, it seems likely that they contain some 2,000 million people out of today's world total of just over 3,000 million.

The second group has the lowest fertility and includes nearly all Western Europe with its highly developed industry and limited space. England and Wales with a rate of 16.4 in 1958; West Germany with 17.0; France with 18.1; Italy and Switzerland, both with 17.4; Sweden with 14.3, are typical members. The Netherlands, Ireland, and the Iberian Peninsula are the only parts of Western Europe with rates above 20 per thousand, and they are not far above. Japan is the only Asian country below this dividing line, with 17.9, and is presumably the only Asian country which qualifies for this group of countries which we characterize as industrialized and crowded. Total population is of the order of 500 million.

The third group consists of countries which are well off and have a good deal of space; they include Canada (27.6), the United States (24.3), Australia (22.6), and New Zealand (25.2). These rose to their present high birth rates during and immediately after World War II, but instead of dropping back in the fifties to the level of the thirties as did most countries of Western Europe, they seem to have established new and stable norms. Their stability is the new feature; during previous history their excess over Western Europe seemed temporary, as though their curve was falling at the same rate but had started at a higher level and not yet caught up. It is conceivable that the USSR belongs with these, at least if we can accept the figure which it reported to the United Nations for 1957 of 25.3 births per thousand population. Including the USSR would make the total population of this third class of countries about 500 million.

We do not conclude that the poor countries are growing faster than the better-off ones, because death rates are higher for the poor countries. Countries with a birth rate of about 40 per thousand, such as India, typically have a death rate of about 20 per thousand, giving them an annual increase of about 2 per cent. This is double the annual natural increase of Western Europe of 1 per cent but is no greater than the increase of the third group of countries. Thus if we disregard migration, Canada with its birth rate of 27.6 per thousand and its death rate of 7.9 (1958) is increasing at the same 2 per cent per year as India. But the poor countries have falling death rates. They may all be approaching the situation of Mexico, with only 12.2 deaths against its 44.5 births per thousand population, a natural increase of 3.23 per cent per year. This is much faster than the natural increase of the rich and spacious countries, and somewhat higher than Canada attains in most years even including immigration.

One could use such international differences between birth and death rates as a point of entry into a discussion of many aspects of economic development, or draw from them conclusions on world politics and economics. But I shall go on to examine one of the group of countries which are spacious and rich—Canada—and try to see how it is accomplishing its alteration from the low fertility of the 1930's to the medium fertility which it shows today.

Between the 1840's and the 1930's the Canadian birth rate seems to have fallen from about 45 per thousand population to about 20 per thousand. Though data are not available for the whole period, it seems certain that in the van of the decline throughout were the better off, the more educated, the more urban. These differences certainly stand out clearly during the last part of the period, for which statistics are available. The 1941 census question asking women how many children they had ever had even permitted the measurement of the degree to which the differential had a spatial dimension; both in Ontario and in Quebec it revealed an average difference of about one child between farm families near the city and farm families far from the city (in favour of the latter) when income and other variables were held constant. Over the ninety-year period the several statistically identifiable groups were passing from a birth rate well above 40 down to one below 20, though few had completed the transition, and some had barely started it, by the late 1930's when the entire process was interrupted. The downward trend of the birth rate suddenly changed to a climb in the over-all figures at about the same pace as the previous decline. The graph of the first thirty years of the official Canadian vital statistics from 1921 to 1951 shows a clear symmetry: about fifteen years of fall and then about fifteen years of rise. At the beginning of the 1920's and at the end of the 1940's the level was about 27 per thousand.

The low point of the 1930's was 1937 when the rate stood at 20.1. We can believe that this is the historical all-time low for Canada, for no reversion to it is in sight. Between 1946 and 1959 there was a degree of stability which cannot be very common in the annals of demography, the lowest year (1950) standing at 27.1, and the highest (1954) at 28.5. (The preliminary 1960 figure, still subject to change is 26.9.) The curve for the white population of the United States is parallel to ours, but about 2 or 3 births per thousand of population lower; thus the 1921–5 average was 25.4; the low point of 17.6 was reached in 1936; the 1946 figure was 23.6, and this is about the level which has been maintained during the past fifteen years.

When this rise in the birth rate of Canada and other western countries was first perceived in the early 1940's, a discussion began which has only recently died down. It revolved around the question of the degree in which the higher births were simply the result of delayed marriages, and delayed births within marriages, the delays being the consequence of economic depression. Once the notion of delay comes into the discussion it is necessary to change the measurement, and to talk not about the trend in births of a particular year in relation to the population in question but about the trend in the number of children that people have in their completed family. Even then there is no final word on how many of the children of the 1940's were simply delayed from the 1930's, and how many were the result of a change in the value system, by which people simply wanted larger families than before. Some of the most sophisticated work in the measurement of this point, which makes use of all that statistical science can tell, is due to a Canadian, Norman Ryder. He argues that we ought not to bring in the value system until we have exhausted the possibilities of explanation offered by statistical data.

One such set of data is the marriage rates. There seems little doubt that a larger proportion of the population gets married now than formerly, and that a larger proportion of marriages take place below the age of 25; either of these circumstances alone would lead to some rise in the birth rate if other things remained equal. In 1931 there were 66,591 marriages in a population of 10,376,786, a rate of 6.4 marriages per thousand of population; in 1958 the figure was 7.7 per thousand.

Perhaps more relevant is the proportion of the population in the child-bearing ages who are married, as given in censuses; in 1956 there were 2,140,000 persons 35–44 years of age, and of these 1,842,000, or 86 per cent, were married; the comparable figure for 1931 was 81 per cent. The average age of brides at first marriage in 1958 was 23.2; in 1940 it was 24.7. Tabulations of the vital statistics according to age at first marriage are not available prior to 1940, but we can compare the average age of all brides; it was 25.5 in 1921, 24.9 in 1931, and 24.8 in 1958.

The distribution by age at marriage has shifted somewhat more than this small change of average would suggest. Out of 131,525 women married in 1958, 94,335 or 72 per cent were under 25 years of age; the corresponding percentage thirty years earlier was 66. We note not only the fact that this is likely to increase the birth rate, since the rate of fertility of women under 25 is particularly high, but also note the tendency to uniformity in the ages at which people decide to get married, a point which will reappear in another framework. One may suppose that in former times the financial position of the man was a more important factor than it is now, with government responsibility for full employment so that husband and wife can work if they find it necessary. This corresponds with increased deliberate spacing of children by couples, the assumption of financial responsibility by the husband presumably coming not at the time of marriage but at the birth of the first child.

There is probably a world-wide trend towards the conversion of marriage from an institution in which the entire community is concerned to one which is primarily the concern of the couples themselves. To most Asians marriage is still too important a matter to be left to the young people; in Canada even the parents of the young people, let alone more distant relatives, have little influence over the choices which are made. It is in accord with the change from institution to companionship that the ages of bride and groom tend to approach one another; in 1940 the bridegrooms of first marriages were, on the average, 3 years and 4 months older than their brides; in 1958 the difference in age was 2 years and 10 months.

It is natural to enquire how much of the increase in the birth rate after World War II is due simply to earlier marriages, that is to say, higher proportions of the population married in the childbearing ages. Allan H. LeNeveu has reported on this in an unpublished memorandum. He compares 1941 and 1956, and considers the crude rate of legitimate births, which rose from 21.2 to 26.7 during the fifteen years. His conclusion is that approximately 70 per cent of the rise was due to

BIRTH RATE PER THOUSAND POPULATION 1921-5

18— 19— 20— 21— 22— 23— 24— 25— 26— 27— 28— 29— 30— 31— 32— 33— 34— 35—

QUE

MAN

SASK NB

ALTA

PEI NS
ONT

BC

25—
26—
27—
28—
29—
30—
BIRTH RATE PER THOUSAND
POPULATION 1959

BIRTHS PER THOUSAND WOMEN 15–44, 1921–5

80— 85— 90— 95— 100— 105— 110— 115— 120— 125— 130— 135— 140— 145— 150— 155—

QUE

SASK

NB

ALTA

MAN

NS

PEI

ONT

BC

125—
130—
135—
140—
145—
BIRTHS PER THOUSAND
WOMEN 15–44, 1959

higher proportions married in the childbearing ages, and only about 30 per cent to higher fertility in marriage.

But the comparison of the birth rate of 1921–5, averaging 27.4 per thousand of population with that of 1959, 27.5 (a level to which it has held very closely since 1946) is one of bald averages that conceals important features of change. Each Canadian figure is the average of several provinces, and it turns out that there have been drastic changes in the provinces relative to one another over the last fifteen years. New Brunswick's birth rate, for instance, stood at 34.0 in 1946 and fell to 27.9 by 1959; British Columbia's rose from 22.5 to 25.5 in the same thirteen years. In the post-war period as well as over the thirty years of the registration records there was a tendency for the rates in formerly "low" provinces to rise and in the "high" to fall; Quebec's dropped from 35.5 in 1921–5 to 28.5 in 1959; Ontario's rose from 23.7 in 1921–5 to 26.4 in 1959.

This process may fairly be called the convergence of the birth rate. The highest province of 1921–5 had nearly double the rate of the lowest province in those years; by 1959 the highest province was only about 20 per cent higher than the lowest (omitting Newfoundland at both dates). If we plot the several provinces on a pair of axes such that the 1921–5 scale is laid out horizontally and the 1959 scale is vertical, then two observations may be made: (1) eight provinces fall in a horizontal ribbon whose width is only 3 per thousand, outside of which is Alberta; (2) there seems to be little correlation between the birth rate of 1921–5 and that of 1959 in the various provinces, except for the effect of Quebec and British Columbia at the two extremes. Notions of relative stability cause one to expect that in such a diagram the points will fall in a band from the upper left of the diagram to the lower right; this is what happens, for instance, when one plots 1921–5 against 1926–30; it happens much less over forty years.

It is of course conceivable that these facts result not from changes in the percentage of the population married, or from the disposition of couples to have children, but simply from the changed proportions of women of childbearing ages in the population. The possibility of this makes the crude birth rate inadequate for our purpose. A measure which meets part of the objection is the fertility ratio obtained by dividing births by numbers of women 15 to 44 years of age. Thus whereas in the province of Ontario the rate increased from 21.0 births per thousand population in 1921–6 to 26.4 in 1959, an increase of 26 per cent, it went from 101.8 births per thousand women 15 to 44 years of age in the earlier period to 126.5, an increase of 24.5 per cent. Despite some differences between crude birth rates and fertility ratios, there is no alteration of the main theme; the highest province in fertility was 86 per cent above the lowest in 1921-5 and only 18 per cent in 1959, when we use fertility ratios; when we use the crude birth rates the two figures are 88 per cent and 20 per cent respectively. In a scatter diagram of fertility ratios plotting 1921-5 against 1959, we find the same horizontal band as using crude birth rates.

However, our interest in the question of the convergence of the birth rates is not satisfied by these provincial averages. What about the situation within the provinces? Are individual families coming to resemble one another in size? One set of data for answering this question is the statistics of birth by order. When the number of births started to rise, it was first births that were principally affected; thus 28.5 per cent of all births were first births in Ontario in 1931 against 37.9 per cent in 1941. Between 1941 and 1951 it was third births that showed the greatest proportional increase, from 13.7 per cent to 18.3 per cent. More recently it has been fourth births in Ontario (and fifth and sixth in Quebec) that have shown the greatest proportional increases. But orders higher than this have fallen strikingly in all provinces; in 1931 in Quebec, for instance, 28.8 per cent of all births were of seventh or higher order; in 1959, 13.1 per cent were of seventh or higher order; the figures for Ontario are 11.4 and 5.5 per cent respectively. It is clear that though the number of children per family is increasing, the distribution is narrowing; the size of families is becoming more uniform.

Another set of data that reveals a convergence in the birth rate is that concerning the formal education of fathers. Thus if we turn to the 1941 census and consider heads of families thirty-five to forty-four years of age, and note the number of resident children under 15 years of age, we find the average for those with one to four years of schooling to be 2.88 children, and with thirteen or more years of schooling to be 1.61 children, a difference of 1.27 children in favour of the heads of families with little schooling. By 1951 the sizes of the two groups had come together by the diminution of the one and the increase of the other, so that the difference was 1.06; we can say that about one-sixth of the differential had disappeared. The differential of income diminished similarly.

Another kind of convergence is taking place: in the ages at which mothers have children. Larger and larger proportions of children are born to mothers under age 35; in 1928 the proportion of births in which the mother was under 35 years of age was 78.0 per cent; in 1958, 84.8 per cent. The proportion of mothers under 30 at the earlier date was 56.4 per cent; at the latter date, 64.3 per cent. The proportion of children born to mothers under 20 also increased, but very slightly, from 5.1 per cent in 1928 to 6.7 per cent in 1958. This tendency to a concentration in the ages of mothers is plainly related to the decline in higher-order births.

One further item must be mentioned before we discuss the consequences for our national life which follow from these circumstances. The decline in the death rate has been steady over thirty years, the male expectation of life at birth increasing by almost exactly three years each decade since 1931 and the female expectation somewhat more rapidly.

As couples marry younger and have their uniform quota of children younger, as their children in turn marry and leave home younger, as mortality declines, the result is an entirely new demographic element in our population: the relatively young couple whose children have grown up and left home. They are not only still alive but young enough to be part of the labour force. In a typical case they might have had their last child at the age of 30, and this last child has now married and left home before the age of 25, so that they start the new phase of their lives before the age of 55. If they are both 55 the chance that they will both be alive fifteen years later at the age of 70 is .54 on the schedule of mortality prevailing in 1956. The number of such people is likely to increase in the future, with consequences not only for the constitution of the labour force but also for the physical structure of our cities. The couples whose children have left home are likely to become restless in the suburbs; they are glad to leave behind their spacious houses and lawns and take apartments; many of the new high-rise and high-rent apartments which are going up in Toronto and other cities will undoubtedly find their tenants among these people. Their actual appearance is, of course, largely in the future; the trends indicated here are now starting and have yet to generate any very large number of such couples. Their effect on the physical appearance of our cities and the future labour force deserves to be studied by means of quantitative projections.

In addition there is a psychological aspect of the change. The principal fact here seems to be that the number of children and their spacing is increasingly a matter of conscious decision by husbands and wives. One would have thought that when choice and personal decision took over from nature, the varying dispositions and inclinations of individuals would show themselves and dispersion would increase; some people would prefer a large family, others a small family or no children at all. This is the opposite of what the statistics show to be happening; all statistically recognizable groups seem to be converging on a norm.

People exercise their increasing freedom to have the same number of children as their neighbours, in the narrow range of two to four, and to have them at the same ages.

At one time it was thought that children were in unsuccessful competition with material goods; that as a couple became wealthier they found it harder and harder to afford children. This was the usual interpretation of the classic differentials of fertility by which as income rose family size fell, both in time and cross-sectionally at a given time. But now a different model is suggested. Howard Roseborough has identified a "standard package" in consumer purchases, a list of consumer goods such as car, television set, suburban house, dishwasher, and so on, which is bought in a certain order as income permits and constitutes standard equipment of the family. Only when income goes up beyond that sufficient for the last item of the list may it appear that individual notions enter or else saving may take place. This standardization of the package ought to be studied further, especially as to the invariance of the sequence. Along with the data presented above it may turn out that children are no longer in competition with consumer goods, but rather a part of the standard package.

Those of us who set more value on people than on goods, who were disheartened by former trends indicating that children tended to lose out in the competition with goods, can now be encouraged by the evidence that children can compete successfully with goods. This is presumably the lesson of our high total birth rate and the disappearance of the inverse relation to income. But on the other hand, the hope we may have had that control gives free play to intrinsic and highly personal differences among individuals is disappointed by the clear evidence that control is used rather to increase one's resemblance to one's neighbours.

THE GROWTH OF POPULATION IN CANADA

Arthur R. M. Lower, F.R.S.C.

MODERN MAN is a measuring animal: he measures most things (except his own individual self) from the small particles to the universe itself. He no longer merely guesses at the age of the earth, but daily comes closer to ascertaining it. He is making a more and more precise chart of the evolution of his own species. He no longer is content with "Old Stone Ages" and "New Stone Ages" but must have their divisions and geographical diffusions. He measures man's increasing control over his environment, over animals and plants, and can tell us within a few decades when the horse arrived in Egypt. He diligently turns up ancient cities, and the spade of the archaeologist extends the reach of the historian. As for the historian, he will hardly admit his own existence until it is possible to discover individuals identifiable by name—when John Smith, so to speak, appears, then history begins—and this is only within the merest fraction of the concept *time*. Yet in our five or six thousand years of recorded history, so much has happened! Civilizations have risen and fallen, and Spenglers and Toynbees make time-charts for the duration of our own, plotting our present age upon them.

In all this immensity, it seems almost presumptuous to call attention to the tiny fragment of human experience to which the title of this paper appears. "The growth of population in Canada" if viewed under the general concept with which so many of the Fellows of the Royal Society are directly or indirectly concerned, the concept *time*, is but a matter of yesterday and one of no great magnitude. And yet it has its place in the human story and moreover is an important part of *our* story, our Canadian story. As part of the human story, it helps us understand the interesting process of how humanity has widened its range and increased its numbers: it is a chapter in human biology as well as in human history, and one of the best documented chapters that we possess. As part of our Canadian story, it is full of information for the economist and the historian and has many things to say to the statesman and man of affairs, even though the chances of such men hearing what it has to say are small.

Just a little over three-and-a-half centuries from the year in which this article is written, 1961, there was not a single white person in what is now Canada: today there are eighteen million. Other countries in the New World have had comparable experiences but with the exception of Australia and New Zealand, in none is the process known with the same degree of intimate detail as in Canada. "The growth of population in Canada" touching as it does a variety of disciplines seems a particularly appropriate subject for a Society whose Fellows represent a wide sector of the circle of learning. Unfortunately a short paper can do no more than summarize and, in this respect, it sacrifices much of the interest of its title: to explore that title thoroughly would be to write a long book which would touch not only the professional pursuit known as demography, but nearly all aspects of the history of Canada as well.

A few general points may be made by way of introduction. Canada, it is frequently proclaimed, is "larger" than the United States. Why, then, the disparity in the two populations? Any intelligent person will give the answer at once: the more favourable environment and greater utilizable resources of the United States. In other words, human beings, like other animals, respond to favourable environments by increasing their numbers: Baffin Land is somewhat larger than California, but it is unlikely ever to sustain as many people as California. No study of Canadian population can be sound which is not informed by knowledge of the Canadian environment. Again, there is human behaviour in this matter of extending the range of the species. There is begetting, there is also death. There are wars, also pestilences. And in our case, as with all New World countries, there is the Old World standing behind us, with its ships and its migrants. Luckily for us pestilence has not been the historic curse, as it has been in most older countries. Of war on its own soil, Canada for two centuries had its share, and within the present century it has participated in four wars abroad. War as a social phenomenon, whether the country was engaged in it or not, has been an important factor in Canada's growth. The country's story is thus not simply one of uninterrupted, peaceful growth as is, for example, Australia's. Nevertheless, from the viewpoint of the demographer alone, which is necessarily narrower than that of the social historian, it is not war and pestilence that hold the primary positions but the quieter, if mathematically complicated, processes of natural increase and migration. The present paper, reflecting the author's interests and qualifications, or, in respect to the technical aspects of demography, lack of them, will attempt to combine the two approaches.

Canada was under the Crown of France until the Treaty of Paris in 1763 gave it to the Crown of England. The history of the country thus falls into two periods. During the French régime, the white population grew from nothing to about 65,000. From first to last, immigration was scanty and it is estimated that, at the utmost, not more than ten thousand people came from Old France to make their homes in New. The exact numbers of those who came, those who stayed, those who returned, there is no means of ascertaining, but it is known that few newcomers arrived after the beginning of the eighteenth century. For practical purposes the entire French stock in Canada and in the northern United States may be taken as descending from the ten thousand, more or less, original immigrants. Here, then, neglecting individual exceptions and thinking of the group alone, is a people, now several millions, highly conscious of their past, united by blood ties and a strong feeling for family relationship, one of the most homogeneous racial units in the civilized world. Compared with the French of Canada, the French of old France are drawn from here, there, and the other place, as are the English. In Europe, if one seeks comparisons, he thinks of the Swedes, who are "aborigines" in as true a sense of the word as well can be arrived at, their blood unmerged with others for untold centuries. In America, there is nothing comparable: Spanish mingled with Indians; English Americans of the original colonies have mingled with everybody. French Canada has mingled with nobody, neither Indians or English: it is itself. Those who seek to penetrate the mysteries of Canadian life, let them begin at this point.

The Conquest made Canada officially English but it remained actually French. Few people of English speech came to the conquered northern country, and those who did settled only in the little cities of Quebec and Montreal. Officials and soldiers came and went. Business men frequently married French wives, thus beginning that process of fusion which has given the two cities a small circle of old families that cross and recross the linguistic and the religious boundaries, old families that have been neither numerous enough nor influential enough to make themselves into a true middle group and which as population has grown have lost what significance they once had. Around them, Conquest or no Conquest, the habitant "made land" and made children. His numbers increased by leaps and bounds: he flourished after the Conquest as he never had before. The English Conquest was the making of French Canada. It bore not only numbers in its train but French Canadian nationalism, too—self-consciousness and all that, in a people, comes from self-consciousness.

There is a simplicity about the story of population in French Canada that is the complete opposite of the utter complexity presented by English. After the Conquest, there were no more French immigrants, except the occasional wanderer. But year by year there was the steady drive of reproduction, with its human tale of "births, marriages, and deaths." On that tale subtler influences, little understood in former days, were playing. The forces of history said "Make good the lost cause," those of religion enjoined the faithful to increase and multiply and, not merely replenish, but occupy, the earth. Yet as men moved up the educational scale, or even into the two cities and the smaller towns, as new staple products bringing more employment were added to the old inadequate fur trade, the gap between births and deaths, wide though it remained, began to decrease. French Canada, like the rest of the world was to feel the forces of the nineteenth and twentieth centuries. Urbanism, a slow ascent for many to middle class status, more education, more health and rather less mere nature, were exerting their usual brakes on the birth rate. To them could possibly be added the political disturbances of the two rebellions of 1837 and 1838, though there is no statistical material to document this, and the heavy emigration to New England which began about the middle of the nineteenth century. "La fièvre aux états-unis," it is said, almost depopulated certain Quebec countrysides. Yet if countrysides were depleted, towns and cities grew: every river had its sawmill and as the nineteenth century changed into the twentieth, the pulpmill and the paper industry came, and with them hydro-electricity. A new Quebec arose in the northwest of the province. Settlement rolled up into the Canadian Shield and where new agricultural lands were available, as around Lake St. John, they were settled. Mining became a major industry. Montreal went into that astronomical growth that still marks it. Quebec, which had stagnated after the end of the old square timber and wooden ship days, took on a new lease of life. Trois Rivières and Sherbrooke became important cities. Textile towns grew up. Classical colleges increased in number. The universities began to flourish. Automobiles, highways and the other mechanical contrivances multiplied. Trade unions appeared. In short, French Canada became more and more subject to the forces of the world about it and its earlier characteristics as a "natural" population were obscured by the rush of modern industrialism and commercialism.

It is not the purpose of this article to bore the reader with statistical details, but to illustrate this three centuries' story of the growth of the French human stock in Canada, a few are necessary. First as to the total immigration into Canada from France during the seventeenth and eighteenth centuries: although no authoritative figures can be cited, various estimates have been made, mostly in an attempt to account for origins within France of the French people of Canada. As might be expected, these show a considerable concentration in the northwestern provinces of old France, particularly Normandy. One estimate places the total immigration, too exactly no doubt, as 9,484.[1] Secondly, by taking the returns of births and deaths and the returns of total population, which were kept systematically in the old French censuses, it is possible to trace the yearly rate of population growth and to find data upon the fertility of the people. The records after 1760 were not as systematically kept and from 1790 to 1831 a gap exists that has not been filled. After 1831, regularity is restored but the distinction is made between "Roman Catholic" and "Protestant" rather than between French and English. From 1926 on we have the modern Federal records of population, births and deaths, by racial extraction. Suitable allowances may in most cases be made for the various changes of classification and in that way a more or less continuous line of growth established for the population of Canada from the 1660's to the present day, together with its birth rates and, with less accuracy, its death rates.

New peoples in new lands have everywhere had high birth rates—if only because most settlers are vigorous young people. The limiting factor is usually the scarcity of women, and what women there are are seldom without either husbands or numerous children. "Les femmes y portent tous les ans," says a French official of the 1660's, referring to women in New France. Demographers seem to think that actual fertility rates may be no higher in the new countries than in the old, but in the new country there is more space, more food, more opportunity. Another way of putting this is in the semi-sociological jargon statement that "high fertility is largely attributable to the high frequency and early age of marriage."[2] The "crude birth rate," that is, the over-all birth rate, for 1665 was about fifty per thousand. Two-and-a-half centuries later, the rate in the purely rural counties of Quebec was not materially different. This rate, high as it was, was to rise still higher, to an average of around fifty-seven during the first half of the eighteenth century, after the defeat of the Iroquois had assured the survival of the French colony and the failure of the English to take Quebec in the War of the Spanish Suc-

[1]*Bulletin des Recherches historiques* (1940), p. 179.
[2]"The Fertility of French Canadian Women During the 17th Century," *Amer. J. Sociol.*, 47, p. 680.

cession had assured the survival of French dominion. During the subsequent period, settlement expanded, there were more food, many more cattle, and much successful fur trade. The population of the colony reflected this in a steady upward trend. During the last period of warfare, the 1750's, the records are not so good, but they indicate, as they should, a fall in the birth rate in the years of actual war and invasion, from 1755 on, and then, a steep post-Conquest rise to just over sixty-five in the middle 1760's. This, if accurate, must surely be an "all-time high" for any considerable community. For the same year, 1765, the deaths returned would give a rate of 45 per thousand. I have heard of no pestilence during that year, so am at a loss to explain the figure: it may cast doubt on the accuracy of that for births.

The influences mentioned above as "brakes on the birth rate" would appear to have begun to operate about the mid-nineteenth century. For 1851, the rate was 45, as against a death rate of 19. A slow fall occurred during the next half of the century and by 1891 the rates were 42 and

TABLE I

GROWTH OF THE FRENCH POPULATION OF CANADA

Year	Population	Birth rate	Death rate	Natural increase	Historical event, etc.
1665	3,215	44	9.8	34.2	First census, under Talon
1675	7,832	50	6	44	
1698	15,355	51	13.8	37.2	Iroquois wars over
1724	26,710	53	22.5	30.5	Inter-war prosperity
1739	42,701	54.9	20	34.9	War about to begin, 1743, thence more or less con-
1739–54	no records				tinuous to 1760
1754	55,009	62.4	31	31.4	Seven Years' War 1756–63

The Province of Quebec: Roman Catholics

1765	69,816	65.6	45	20.6	Non-French Catholics
1790	134,374	50.9	31	19.9	negligible in numbers
1790–1831	no records				

The Province of Lower Canada: Roman Catholics

1831	412,717	50	28	22	A small number of non-
1851	746,851	45	19	26	French Roman Catholics coming in

The Province of Quebec: Roman Catholics

1871	1,019,887	43.3	20.5	22.8	First post-Confederation census
1901	1,430,776	41	19	22	Rates for 1901 by inter-polation

Persons of French Origin: Quebec

1931	2,270,000	36.4	12.5	23.9	First period in which racial, not religious,
1951	3,327,000	31.4	8.4	23.0	classification given

22. By 1901, they had become 37 and 19. From 1926 on, birth and death rates by racial origin are available through the Annual Reports on Vital Statistics. In 1931, they work out at 36.4 and 12.5. For 1951, they were 31.4 and 8.4. I inflict on the reader Table I, giving birth and death rates at approximately equal intervals.

This is the longest and probably the most accurate account in the world of population growth. I believe figures for Sweden, Europe's earliest, begin in 1750. For all other European countries, until the nineteenth century there are estimates only. The first census of the United States was not taken until 1790. The data compiled by the French authorities are consistent within themselves over the century during which they were kept: the English were more casual, and it is unfortunate that the long gap exists between 1790 and 1831. The fact that the term "Roman Catholic" is more inclusive than "French" makes only a minor difference, in that non-French Roman Catholics have never constituted more than a small fraction of the Catholic people of Quebec. Although the French birth rate of 1951, 31.4, was much lower than in previous years, it was still much higher than that of the English, which would be about 20. Since the French death rate, thanks to modern health measures, has now become less than that of the English (who do not die of disease much more, but must die of old age) the French population is now a young, and presumably buoyant, population: the English Canadians are a much older people on the average than are the French. This relative age composition may not always exist unchanged. But, urbanized or not, the French people of Canada are still increasing at about the same rate as their ancestors two hundred years ago. Since they have proceeded out of the bodies of around ten thousand people, their present millions are, in their own sense of the word, all "parents," alike physically and psychologically, one of the most closely-knit blood clans of the western world.

When we turn to English Canada, we find a picture as different as well could be. Instead of simplicity, complexity; instead of a straight-line development, innumerable eddies in the stream; instead of homogeneity, the extremes of diversity. Geographically English Canada takes its rise from several settlements, not one or two. Ethnically, its people from the beginning are drawn from several stocks. These have no religious unity and little occupational. Traditions and ways of life are many. People come and go, not in a total of a few thousands but in many thousands: immigration from the ends of the earth becomes a social phenomenon of the first magnitude.

English Canada as we now know it begins in Newfoundland, goes on

with Nova Scotia, with Quebec, with Prince Edward Island, New
Brunswick and Upper Canada. After a long interval, it reaches the
Prairies and the Pacific coast. The first Newfoundland settlers were from
the west of England and from Catholic Ireland. Then in Nova Scotia
there were Germans, New Englanders, Catholic Irish, Scots, more
English. Loyalists came. After the Napoleonic Wars a mass immigration
from the British Isles poured into all the provinces, but the weight
of it fell on Upper Canada. In the 1870's the first waves of a new
European immigration began and though marked by a series of pulsations, these have never ceased. So varied has been the stream of new
life that some may be disposed to question the use of the very words
English Canada. English Canada is that part of Canada which is not
French, it may be said. The term is convenient and apart from strict
ethnic origins, it has a substantial reality, for the English language and
English institutions have made or are making a unity of all those who
come to the country, whatever their origin. I shall continue to use it.

Nova Scotia began in ethnic diversity. The settlers of Halifax (1749)
were a mixed lot. They were soon joined by the Lunenburgers (1753):
one of the first waves of English settlement thus was German. Then
came New Englanders (1758), and a little later Scots of both varieties,
people from Yorkshire, and at the end of the American Revolutionary
war (1783), some United Empire Loyalists from many colonies. In the
early nineteenth century further important quotas came from the Scottish
Highlands, and not unnegligible numbers from other parts of the British
Isles. Each of these groups settling in different areas, except the English,
formed communities whose outlines are still plainly visible. But by
about 1825, the province had received the bulk of its newcomers and
it has since grown much as French Canada has grown, from within itself.
For over a century past it has been a province of emigration, rather than
of immigration.

The Conquest did not result in any considerable influx of English-
speaking people into the Province of Quebec, and not until the cities
of Quebec and Montreal became large ports of export, roughly, that is,
by about 1800, did any important number of English-speaking people
come to live in them. By about the year 1840 the province had received
as high a proportion of people of English speech as it was ever to have.
Today the ratios between the two languages seem stable and in the
proportion of about four to one.

It was into the two new provinces of New Brunswick and Upper
Canada that the first large wave of English-speaking newcomers was to
come. This was the influx of United Empire Loyalists. By modern
standards their numbers were not great—fifteen thousand more or less

to New Brunswick, and rather fewer than ten thousand to Upper Canada—but the two new provinces were their provinces and they put a permanent mark on both. New Brunswick today is a composite province, but its St. John valley, below Woodstock, remains much what it has always been, a Loyalist community, with Loyalist attitudes. It took rather less than a generation for the settlers in Upper Canada to make themselves into a new *British American* community, one with its own characteristics, characteristics that were to be hardened and pointed in the War of 1812.

In so far as racial derivation goes, the Loyalists too were a mixed lot. In Upper Canada, those of German or New York Dutch origin were numerous. Others were Gaelic-speaking Highlanders, some were English, some from Ulster and some native Americans of English origin. All brought with them something more significant to the future than ethnic origin or even the remains of non-English speech: they brought the determination to make good a lost cause, not to knuckle under to their former compatriots, to balance the New World with the Old across the seas. It is these attitudes transmitted and extended to others over the generations which have been the influential Loyalist contribution to the modern country.

The Loyalist migration was typical of the way in which population has grown in English Canada. A large new element came into the country within a short period and new communities arose quite different from the old. These had to build up their life from nothing and find appropriate modifications for the old institutions. Almost immediately the skeleton in the Canadian population closet began showing itself, for no sooner had the Loyalists got into their new homes than many of them drifted away again, south over that border from below which they had come. Their descendants continue to do so. There never has been a group of immigrants into Canada of which this has not been true.

A second example of the same type of community building is afforded by the experience of Upper Canada in the generation after the Napoleonic Wars, say from 1820 to 1850. In this period, a large immigration set in from all parts of the British Isles and, at the end of it, the old Loyalist community of Upper Canada had been submerged. A new Upper Canada had come into existence, with new men, new towns, new ideas. For the rise of this new Upper Canada, we have an enormous collection of travellers' impressions and books of advice to immigrants as well as numbers of books recording settlers' experiences, such as Mrs. Moodie's classic *Roughing it in the Bush*. There is also a good store of statistical material. Comment on literary portrayals of settlement must be beyond the scope of this paper. But a summary of statistical results may be presented. I have devoted a few pages in my *Canadians in the Making* to the peopling of Upper Canada after the War of 1812 (chapter 14) and those who wish more extended comment may find it there. Here what I would like to do is to expand the material which I there gave in a mere footnote (p. 209) thereby offering a demographic and mathematical problem for solution by others more competent than myself.

We are fortunate in having censuses for Upper Canada for nearly every year from 1824 on. We also have various statements of emigration from the United Kingdom, and rather fewer of immigration into Canada by way of the St. Lawrence. Modern authorities have republished statistics, with their own comments and collations. The information we have of births and deaths in the period enables us to hazard figures for the natural increase year by year from 1824 to 1851. Thus the Census of 1851, first of the Decennial Censuses of Canada, which may be read back into previous years, in addition to population gives births and deaths. The 1851 return points to a natural increase year by year of about 25 per 1000, a high rate, but not too high for a pioneer country, where new land was abundant, towns few and small, and the proportion of young, vigorous, and lusty rural folk large. In addition to these objective statistics, it is necessary to have, as it were, "the feel" of Upper Canada in the period, something to which the Canadian historian perhaps may lay claim. From all these sources, it is possible to make a table that gives a fair picture of the way in which Upper Canada grew numerically when it was a new province. Such a table can only be approximate, but it comes out fairly well and "'twill serve" (Table II).

The table requires us to face the fact that we have failed to account for nearly 100,000 people (952,000 — 854,000). We have put down all the immigrants who arrived by the St. Lawrence and have added a fairly large quota each year for natural increase: the natural increase is approximately compounded, being based on the figures for the year or years before. We are still short our hundred thousand that the Census of 1851 assures us were in Upper Canada. Where had they come from? There is one possibility: a heavy immigration into Upper Canada from the United States. It is known that many British immigrants did come to Upper Canada via New York (the great George Brown did, for example, but as an immigrant he was not George Brown, just a "statistic"). Many are known to have made the journey in the opposite direction. Were the people of the time even more prolific than the figure struck for "natural increase" assumes?

Again resorting to statistics, it is possible to suggest strongly that there was a large emigration from the province. Table III illustrates.

TABLE II

CALCULATED AND ACTUAL POPULATION OF UPPER CANADA 1824–51

Year	Population by census	Probable natural increase	Immigration via the St. Lawrence	Expected population in the next year	Actual population for the next year
1824	151,000	4,000	6,000	161,000	158,000(−)*
1825	158,000	4,000	6,000	168,000	163,000(−)
1826	163,000	4,000	8,000	175,000	176,000(+)*
1827	176,000	4,000	8,000	188,000	185,000(−)
1828	185,000	5,000	8,000	198,000	
1829	no census	5,000	9,000	212,000	
1830	,, ,,	5,000	21,000	238,000	
1831	,, ,,	6,000	40,000	284,000	261,000(−)
1832	261,000	7,000	46,000	337,000	
1833	no census	7,000	19,000	364,000	320,000(−)
1834	320,000	8,000	28,000	356,000	336,000(−)
1835	336,000	8,000	10,000	354,000	
1836	no census	9,000	23,000	386,000	
1837	,, ,,	10,000	21,000	417,000	385,000(−)
1838	385,000	10,000	3,000	398,000	407,000(+)
1839	407,000	10,000	8,000	425,000	427,000(+)
1840	427,000	11,000	22,000	460,000	465,000(+)
1841	465,000	12,000	28,000	505,000	486,000(−)
1842	486,000	12,000	37,000	535,000	
1843	no census	13,000	16,000	564,000	
1844	,, ,,	14,000	15,000	593,000	
1845	,, ,,	15,000	23,000	631,000	
1846	,, ,,	16,000	30,000	677,000	
1847	,, ,,	17,000	76,000	770,000	723,000(−)
1848	723,000	18,000	22,000	763,000	
1849	no census	19,000	29,000	811,000	
1850	,, ,,	20,000	23,000	854,000	952,000(+)
1851	952,000				

*(−) = less than expected   (+) = more than expected

TABLE III

IMMIGRATION FROM THE BRITISH ISLES TO THE PROVINCE OF CANADA, 1815–51, COMPARED WITH PERSONS BORN ABROAD BUT LIVING IN CANADA ACCORDING TO THE CANADIAN CENSUS

	Immigration		Deaths		Remainder		Residents born abroad		Unaccounted for
1815–42	450,000	−	50,000	=	400,000	−	242,000	=	158,000
1842–51	345,000								
1815–51	795,000	−	100,000	=	695,000	−	428,000	=	267,000

In the table I admit to having taken the liberty of assuming the deaths of fifty thousand of the immigrants of 1815–42 and of fifty thousand more of those who came from 1842 to 1851. Since immigrants are usually young and since the death rate in Canada was not overly high, even in those days, I think I have been unduly hard on the immigrant population. However, I wish to make the point: a very large number of the immigrants reported as coming to Canada, 1815–51, were not to be found there in 1851, and the presumption is that they had either returned home or gone on to the United States. This has been the invariable Canadian experience. The only way I can see of reconciling the two tables is to presume a much higher native born rate of natural increase than I had allowed for in Table II, 25 per 1000 per annum. It seems probable that much of the heavy immigration into pioneer Upper Canada was impermanent but those who stayed we know had large families. These latter were the permanent immigrants. One thinks of the statement made some years ago by the Hon. J. W. Pickersgill that the most satisfactory immigrant is the one that comes by way of nature— a statement that proved most unpopular among a people like English Canadians, who appear to distrust and dislike nothing so much as themselves.

By 1851 the great rush into Upper Canada was slackening, by 1860 it had ceased. There was good reason for this: the most desirable lands had been taken up. A large number of people continued to terminate the ocean voyage at the port of Quebec, but they did not even hover in Upper Canada: they were nearly all mere transients, on their way to the western states. For the period from about 1860 to about 1890 immigrants who came to Canada and did not pass on to the United States either bought farms from previous settlers or sought the towns. There was not much extension of settlement, for there could not be, except in the rough lands of the Canadian Shield, and there was a notable pause in the general pace of development. The major new resources were the pine lumber of the back country east and north of the great lakes, and the slowly opening lands of western Canada. Not until railway transport had opened the west and new species of wheat had overcome its short seasons could there be a repetition of the experience of Upper Canada. Consequently immigrants did not so much add to the population as displace the native born. The period was one of heavy emigration to the United States, especially to those states such as the Dakotas, where free homesteads were still obtainable. Some areas of the American west were populated almost entirely by Canadians, whose descendants have long since been Americans. Sir Richard Cartwright put the disappointments of the period in a phrase when he labelled it as "beginning in Lamentations and ending in Exodus." The 1850's had been the most prosperous decade the colonies had known, or were to know, until a repetition of the same causes gave Canada another and similar experience at the opening of the twentieth century.

Railways, new wheats, large markets for wheat, rising prices, these were the big items in the prosperity of the early twentieth century. Their products having assured markets, the new lands of the west played the same part as those of Upper Canada had played three-quarters of a century before. People were attracted to them, especially when there were homesteads to be had for nothing, or more attractive still, money to be "made" out of the homesteaders. Added to these things was the filling up of the good lands of the northern states, and the consequent deflection of a portion of the American wave of immigration northward. The peoples had come to the Republic in a natural order: those who were nearest came first. Emigration to America began from the British Isles, moved on to Germany, Scandinavia, and the Mediterranean and ended up with the eastern Slavs. Canada got fragments from the first of these waves and from the last. Her early immigrants came from the British Isles with a few from Germany. She missed the Scandinavian nineteenth-century waves and much of the Mediterranean. But she received, beginning about 1890, a considerable proportion of the Slavic. That is merely the broad picture. A number of Germans had come in the first half of the century to reinforce the German–North Americans of Waterloo County, Ontario, and in the 1870's, there came more—this time Mennonites, who went to Manitoba. At the same time, the first contingents of Icelanders arrived.

The heavy immigration from the European continent which has been so marked a feature of Canadian life down to the present, and Asiatic immigration, did not become significant until about the turn of the century. It is Sir Clifford Sifton who is usually credited, or discredited, with the energy and policies that were once more to upset the community which had been forming in Canada and to require the creation of still another. Sifton's "peasant in a sheepskin coat, with a fat wife and ten children" has become the classical image of the immigrants who came into Canada, literally in millions, during the period from 1896 to the beginning of World War I. This Sifton immigration constituted another in the series of "pulsations" by which Canada's population growth has been characterized. It filled the West as rapidly as, but not more rapidly than, the immigration of 1815–50 had filled Upper Canada. While there was a proportion of the old British stock within it, it differed fundamentally from the earlier immigration in providing the country with a new population entirely different from its older neighbours in languages, traditions, social customs, and religion. We are still digesting this Siftonian immigration: it may be that the arrival of one of its representatives, in 1958, at cabinet rank indicates that the process is past its period of greatest stress.

After World War I, the assumption, on the part of the ministry of the day, of business men, of promoters, and of others who knew nothing about what happens in immigration, was that the Siftonian tide would flow again and towards its former objective, the land: it was forgotten that there were no more empty Saskatchewans. And flow the tide did, though hardly in its first volume. Down to 1930 over twelve hundred thousand immigrants entered Canada but relatively few went on the land (there was not much land left for them to go on) and, when the count was taken in 1931, less than half of them remained. Shortly after the beginning of his ministry, R. B. Bennett, desperately fighting The Depression (it is proper to capitalize the words), turned off the immigration tap: from 1931 until its resumption under Mr. King in 1946, the stream ceased to flow. Then, just after the war, the King government, responding to the pressure of "promotion," as had the Laurier government before it, once more opened the gates. Another pulsation resulted which, from that time to this, has been continuous. In round numbers in the fifteen years from 1946 to 1961, something like two million immigrants have come to Canada. The interesting question is "How many have remained?" No answer can be given until the results of the 1961 census become available.

In summary, since the beginnings in the seventeenth century, we have had six major waves of immigration. The first was that which gave a settled population to New France and assured the survival of the colony, small in numbers but of crucial importance in determining the nature of the future. The second was the Loyalist immigration, equally significant in determining the future. The third was the wave from the British Isles after 1820, which gave to Upper Canada an entirely new character, though one which did not involve linguistic changes or changes in the conception of political allegiance. The fourth was the Siftonian immigration of 1896–1914, which greatly speeded up the process of populating the west and brought into Canada a third element, neither British nor French, a composite element made up of innumerable peoples with innumerable languages, religions, and views of the nature of the state. The fifth continued this wave but was much more urban in its direction. The sixth consisted in the post-war immigration, which greatly added to the numbers of "the stranger within our gates." These "strangers" differed in important particulars from those who had come earlier. Before 1930, most of the recently arrived Germanic people in Canada were a simple peasantry; they were also *Auslandsdeutsch* and as such not really Germans. Since the last war, Canada has received a large contingent of *Reichsdeutsch*, and many of these have been people of education: they may be presumed to have brought with them to Canada that degree of efficiency which during the war repeatedly made the allied soldiery look like amateurs. Again, before 1945, and even beyond that year, the Canadian government's criterion of a good immigrant was one with a strong back: farm labourers and servant girls were the preferred classes. This peculiar standard of excellence has slowly and covertly been abandoned since 1945, with the result that Canadians in leading positions now often find themselves in the presence of immigrants of a culture superior to their own, no doubt both an unlooked-for and unwelcome upshot. Thirdly, as a result of the war, Canada has become an asylum for the distressed, the displaced, the political refugee, and those who cannot stomach the oppressions and despotisms of the afflicted parts of the old world. Nothing is more admirable than those Viking voyages made by tiny shiploads of men, women, and children from some Baltic port, people securing, say, a yacht, stealing away by night, facing the Atlantic in their tiny ships, bound for a land of freedom. Such episodes will have a continuing place in the Canadian story: they will be more valuable than millions of mere peasants in sheepskin coats. And let us hope that the people who have had the courage to find us out in this way will not all emigrate to the United States.

The results of immigration can be assessed from almost every human standpoint. We must think of the effects of transplantation on the immigrant, his success or failure, the gifts or disabilities which he brings, the effects on the society and the economy to which he comes, the cheapness or docility of labour which must mark him, his fertility as compared with the older stocks, his average social and education level, his political baggage (how does the immigration officer get at that?), his religion or the absence thereof, the attitude of the society into which he comes, and, more technically, whether immigration, except under special circumstances, does in reality increase the rate of population growth or not. Here it is quite impossible to paint in such a large canvas: one or two passing observations at most may be made.

The immigrant who comes to a new country must either sink or swim. His position is well expressed in the line: "No retreat, no retreat: they must conquer or die who have no retreat." The native inhabitant, however, sees the newcomer in a cold light. He is a competitor, he is different, he eats different food, thinks different thoughts, and, to the world's worst linguists (the English Canadians, or do I need explain?), he is obviously making unpleasant remarks about themselves in a language which they have no intention of understanding. The result must necessarily be tension, open or concealed:

> The stranger within my gates
> He may be evil or good
> But I cannot tell what powers control,
> What reasons sway his mood
> Nor when the gods of his far-off land
> May repossess his blood.
> The men of my own stock
> Bitter bad they may be
> But at least they hear the things I hear
> And see the things I see.
> And whatever I think of the likes of them
> They think of the likes of me.

The poet (Rudyard Kipling) expresses a sentiment no longer fashionable. But fashion does not have the last word in human relationships. Every large infusion of new blood, even of the old stock, even from the British Isles, causes social difficulties which may take years in disappearing. The further removed from the mass of the population, the longer the time for the difficulties to disappear. In times of swelling economic life, everybody rides along on the same wave of prosperity and it is not necessary to notice the presence of newcomers. Let hard times come and a different note is soon heard. The analysis should go much further than it can be carried here. It should especially consider the attitudes towards the state and towards humanity in which we English-speaking people believe (and which constitute almost our sole claim to merit), which may or may not be shared (but seldom understood) by the newcomer and the length of time it may take him and his children to become in the full sense a member of the society to which he finds himself introduced. Here is a field in which the shallow thinker has had nearly the whole game to himself in Canada. Our attitude towards population has simply been that of members of "The Boosters' Club," "bigger and bigger," has been virtually the only criterion. This attitude differs little, however, from that of the economist, who has approached an intensely human problem from an abstract, materialistic angle. The economist would possibly defend himself by saying that he is not looking at the problem in other than the terms of his own discipline and that this necessarily leads him to think of immigration in terms of the production of wealth. The social and human aspects of immigration, he might say, are beyond his field. But economists often are not hesitant in suggesting policy and, in doing so, they take on responsibilities much wider than those concerned only with "the production and distribution of wealth," responsibilities which they are not qualified, *qua* economists, to assume.

No technical talk about the production of wealth can disguise the intensely human aspects, the crucial aspects, of immigration. We probably should not talk about the abstraction "immigration," but rather about the immigrant. For, behind every immigrant, there looms potential tragedy. He comes to a new land and, sooner or later, he has to shed his old self, make himself over again, literally be born again. Between him and his children a gulf opens, often an uncrossable gulf. Under such circumstances, I would prefer one J. S. Woodsworth in his "All Peoples' Mission" to a hundred theorists talking about "the absorptive capacity of the economy."

Canadian authority, for the most part, has seen through the eyes of those who talk about the absorptive capacity of the economy and has regarded the immigrant as an abstraction who only becomes a human being when he becomes a nuisance. With the development of the Citizenship Branch of the Department of Immigration, a different attitude is becoming discernible, though it is as yet by no means the dominant one. Official propaganda has traditionally represented this country as a land flowing with milk and honey: it has rarely had the courage to face our realities. As I have just said, the deepest reality for the immigrant is this matter of having to make himself over again into a new man, with a new language, new habits, new attitudes towards life, politics, society, culture. No immigrant can escape this process: he cannot live to himself alone and if he lives in a colony of his fellows, sooner or later that colony begins to crumble. If colonies could hold out and maintain indefinitely their own way of life, together with their language, we would have a Balkanized country that would sooner or later fall apart in racial division: surely one does not need to offer illustrations of this world-wide phenomenon. Yet we have the Citizenship Branch offering this sentimental mush as "policy":

The Citizenship Branch has based its integration program on the premise that Canadian culture will be enriched and strengthened by diversity. . . . From the very beginning of Canada's history as a nation the principle of acceptance of religious, cultural and social differences has been recognized.

The influx of immigrants from many ethnic backgrounds has added cultural variety without changing this basic principle. At the same time all Canadians share a common citizenship within a common framework of government and democratic institutions. . . . In keeping with the democratic belief in the dignity and freedom of the individual, it is felt that integration should be voluntary and should not be pressed. It is assumed that integration should be moderate in its demands on the immigrant and less painful for him than assimilation would be. . . . [There follows an attempt at a fine-spun distinction between "integration" and "assimilation."][3]

There is good intention in the statement, that is obvious, and something may be perhaps said for "diversity" providing the word is not taken too seriously. But surely this scholastic attempt to draw a line between "integration" and "assimilation" will fool no one, least of all the immigrant. Of course the immigrant has to be assimilated, or assimilate himself, of course he has to lose his racial and linguistic, if not his personal, identity. Not long ago, I was in the home of a German immigrant, of professional status. His English was still poor, but his children were talking in just the same accent as that used by the author of this paper; when they grow up, their German will recede farther and farther and their own children will understand only a few words: they will have become assimilated. The process has been repeated millions of times in North America: it takes approximately three generations.

Then let us face that fact: let us remember that immigration, to the immigrant, is a profound personal experience and to the state, since into a community already formed it introduces numbers of persons of dislocated life, a political and social problem comparable with those posed by a major war.

This paper is not intended to be a sociological treatise, though many such are needed on the subject, but rather a semi-statistical analysis. Two large points, therefore, remain to be made. The first is that the recent period during which we had no immigration, 1931–45, provides a rich mine for those who wish to know how non-native groups behave demographically when they are not continually reinforced by immigrants from the land from which they came. It may be dismissed briefly. Again let me refer to my *Canadians in the Making*, this time to chapters 24 and 25, especially 25, where I have tried to analyse the available statistics. Suffice it to say here that all statistical evidence points in the one direction, namely, that without continuing immigration, the foreign stocks quickly accommodate themselves to Canadian norms: death

[3]*Canada Year Book*, 1959, p. 177.

rates fall, birth rates fall, the "mother tongue" quickly shrinks in importance and lastly, intermarriage begins.

The second large point has to do with the growth of our population through natural increase and through immigration: it consists in an attempt to estimate the respective contributions through striking a balance sheet of the population for a given ten-year census period. The census gives us birthplaces of the population, total numbers, ethnic origin, and many other types of information. We have the figures for immigration year by year. What we lack are the figures for emigration, which the Canadian authorities have never had the courage to collect. Until they find it (and these would not be impossible figures to collect, since leaving the country is almost as big a decision as coming to it), we have only the information provided by the returns of other countries. Of these the most important is the United States. Many immigrants must return home: others go to the United States. In fact, one of the chief reasons for immigrating to Canada is the prospect of being able to get into the United States. Our own citizens also emigrate to the United States. From American sources we have (*a*) the numbers of the Canadian-born, French, and "other," living in the United States at the time of the taking of the American census, and (*b*) annual returns of immigrants from Canada, Canadian-born and other. There is no reason to distrust the approximate accuracy of American immigration returns. The United States is not an easy country to get into: there are many formalities, and when the right of entrance is granted, something valuable has been obtained. The emigrant from Canada does not just hop backward and forward across the border: when he leaves us, he goes to stay. The reverse is not the case. Our immigration returns show many Americans coming here year by year, but the number of Americans in Canada does not increase: the inference must be that those who come just meet the number of those who die and that there is a return movement back. Save for a stable nucleus, like the Alberta rural immigrants of the 1900's, Americans live in Canada as transients: they are our technicians and managers, doing a turn of garrison duty in this northern hinterland before returning home.

It is much too complex for the present writer to attempt to work out the fine balance between the immigrants of the "x" racial groups who come here and a portion of whom move on to increase the numbers of their respective groups in the United States and then to correlate these with annual American immigration statistics. It is not too difficult, however, to present ten-year population balance sheets that will give some idea of the general and permanent situation. Since the laws

TABLE IV

CANADA: POPULATION "BALANCE SHEET" 1921–31, 1941–51
(All figures to closest thousand)

A. COLLECTED TOTALS

1921–31		1941–51	
Population 1921	8,788	Population 1941	11,507
1931	10,376	1951	14,009
Increase	1,588	Increase	2,502
Population 1921	8,788	Population 1941	11,507
Natural increase 1921–30	1,325	Natural increase 1951	1,963 +
		Newfoundland	348
Immigration 1921–30	10,113 / 1,234		2,311
		Immigration 1941–51	13,818 / 516
Anticipated population 1931	11,347	Anticipated population 1951	14,334
Actual population 1931	10,376	Actual population 1951	14,009
Loss or leakage	970	Loss or leakage	325

B. ELEMENTS IN THE "BALANCE SHEET"

(a) *The Native-Born*
(i) *Total of native-born*

	1921	1931	Increase	1941	1951	Increase	Increase without Newfoundland
French origin	2,368	2,851	483	3,407	4,251	844	844
British origin	3,650	4,017	367	4,562	5,632	1,070	722
Other origins	840	1,189	449	1,519	2,067	548	548
Total	6,858	8,057	1,199	9,488	11,850	2,462	2,111
Natural increase (Vital St. Rep.)			1,325			2,311	2,282
plus Newfoundland							
Native-born unaccounted for			−126			−151	−168

TABLE IV (cont'd)

(ii) Canadian-born in the United States

	1920	1930	Increase	Decrease		1940	1950		Decrease
Approx. deaths (at 12 per M)	1,118	1,279	161		Approx. deaths (at 12 per M)	1,044	995		−49
			144						100
Approx. total Canadian immigration to U.S.			305		Approx. total Canadian immigration to U.S.				51
Canadian-born Death among	1,118				Canadian-born Death among	1,044			
	144					100			
Remainder Immigration (American returns)	974				Remainder Immigration (American returns)		944		
	109						144		
Canadian-born, calculated total	1,083				Canadian-born calculated total		1,088		
Census total	1,289				Census total		995		
Discrepancy	+196				Discrepancy		−93		

(b) The Non-Native-Born

(i) Total of persons born out of the country

Born in	1921	1931	Increase	Decrease	Born in	1941	1951	Increase	Decrease
British Isles	1,065	1,184	119		British Isles	960	912		−48
United States	374	344		−30	United States	312	282		−30
Elsewhere*	516	780	264		Elsewhere*	747	866	119	
	1,955	2,308	353			2,019	2,060	41	

TABLE IV (cont'd)

(b) The Non-Native-Born (cont'd)

(ii) Estimated deaths among immigrants

	1921–31		1941–51
British born	113	British born	100
U.S. born	32	U.S. born	30
Born elsewhere	72	Born elsewhere	82
Total immigrant deaths	217	Total immigrant deaths	212

(iii) Immigration and emigration

	1921–31		1941–51
Immigration from		Immigration from	
British Isles	490	British Isles	224
Europe	505	Europe	222
American citizens	222	American citizens	60
All other	17	All other	9
	1,234		515

*"Elsewhere" includes "other Commonwealth" and Asia, both of which decreased in the later of the two periods. "Elsewhere" substantially is "Europe."

TABLE IV (cont'd)

C. IMMIGRATION AND ACTUAL NUMBERS OF IMMIGRANTS COMPARED

1921-31

	Immigration	Apparent increase	Deaths	Actual increase	Per cent retained
British	490	119	113	232	47
American	222	-30	32	-2	0.9
Other	505	264	72	336	66
Totals	1,234	353	+217 =	570	46

1941-51

	Immigration	Apparent increase	Deaths	Actual increase	Per cent retained
British	224	-48	100	76	34
American	60	-30	30	—	00.0
Other	222	119	82	201	90
Totals	516	41 +	212 =	253	00

D. ALTERNATIVE BREAKDOWN OF DATA IN C

(a)

Immigrant born	1921	1931	Deaths among	Remaining	Immigration	Total born abroad			
						Calculated	Actual	Loss	Per cent
Totals	1,955	2,308	217	1,738+	1,234 =	2,972	2,308	664	54
British	1,065	1,184	113	952+	490 =	1,442	1,184	258	52.6
American	374	344	32	342+	222 =	564	344	220	98.9
Other	516	780	72	444+	505 =	1,021	780	241	47.7

(b)

Immigrant born	1941	1951	Deaths among	Remaining	Immigration	Total born abroad			
						Calculated	Actual	Loss	Per cent
Totals	2,019	2,060	212	1,807+	515 =	2,322	2,060	262	51.8
British	960	912	100	860+	224 =	1,084	912	172	76.6
American	312	282	30	282+	60 =	342	282	60	100.00
Other	747	866	82	665+	231 =	978	866	112	48.4

governing our population growth are in a sense natural laws, they have always been the same. Consequently, whether we select one decade or another does not matter very much, with the important exception that any one decade deserves to be studied in its own right. It will be of interest to present the results of an examination of two post-war decades, 1921–31 and 1941–51. Although we cannot arrange to have wars neatly coincide with the Canadian census decades, these two at least have this in common that they both witness the rush away from a half-destroyed old world to a prosperous new. In order to avoid cluttering up the text I present my analysis, my "balance sheets," separately, as Table IV and let me again warn the reader that I write this paper, not as a professional demographer, but as an amateur, whose ability to apply mathematics to statistical analysis is limited to the four simple rules. Moreover, the human animal is much more lively than the dollar and consequently it is impossible to pin him down as accurately. No "Population Balance Sheet" can have the accuracy of the accountant's: the best that can be expected is an approximation.

For those who do not wish to get involved in examining the tables in detail, the following major points may be set down:

In each decade there was much immigration, a million and a quarter after World War I, and over half a million after World War II.

There was a large surplus in each case of births over deaths.

The actual population as revealed by the census of the end of the decade came nowhere close to equalling the immigration added to this natural increase. The assumption must be that many of the immigrants who are brought here go away again.

The official figures show a large immigration from the United States. All these American immigrants go away again. There is no net immigration from the United States, though presumably much substitution of this American citizen for that one. The Canadian government's figures for American immigration are worthless.

In the two periods under examination, only about half of the immigrants from the British Isles remained in the country.

In the first period about half of those who came from Europe remained in the country. In the second nearly all of them did.

There have been only two decades in our history when the Canadian-born population of the United States has not shown an increase. One of these was the decade of World War I, 1910–20. The other was the decade of World War II, 1940–50.

It should be remembered that when the American census reports an increase, shall we say, of a thousand Canadians living in the

United States over the ten-year period, there must be added to these a number sufficient to substitute for those who die during the period. The true emigration, then, from Canada to the United states is not x thousands but x plus y thousands. The same holds good for immigrants to Canada: to get the true picture, allowance must be made for those who die during the period. Note also that an "immigrant" is not merely a recent arrival, but anyone who was born abroad. Note too that persons going from Canada to the United States include great numbers of non-native Canadians: of such persons it is virtually impossible to keep track, except by comparing the Canadian census results one with another, then making allowance for deaths.

The general picture which emerges from these two balance sheets and from the one presented in Table II for Upper Canada is one of a rush of humanity to take possession of a new land. If the new land be spacious, its soil, climate, and other economic aspects good, then the newcomers will spill out over it, get their living out of it, marry young, if for no other reason than to produce helpers, and have large families, with relatively low death rates. It is in this way that population shoots up quickly in a new country. The experience of Upper Canada and of the Canadian west was similar in this respect.

If the new land available is filled up or economic opportunities fail, as they did in Canada in 1930, then immigration simply slips away. People go somewhere, back home, wherever that may be, or over the southern border, where there always seems room for one more. The vast army of immigrants that came into Canada after 1920 was mostly lost to this country, and in going it took away with it much of its own progeny. And the population growth of the West cut off abruptly at the same time: its curve had risen sharply to 1930, thereafter it became just about horizontal. What happens in these periods of exodus cannot be described statistically. No doubt a cross-section of the population is carried away, drawn from recent and still unsettled newcomers but also from every other type of person, home-grown and imported. One tendency may be assumed—it could be corroborated by individual examples, but not statistically: that is, not only in times of depression but at any time, the cheap man will drive out the dear man. This is what I have elsewhere called the "Gresham's Law of Immigration," after the well-known monetary law by which cheap money drives out dear (the moment the American dollar was depreciated in terms of the Canadian, people began to try to work off their American silver; now that the situation has changed they keep it). Men are something like money: the man who asks the least from life is like the depreciated coin—he has the best chance of circulating. One must adjust the rule, naturally, to all the complexities of humanity, but in general it will hold. The immigrant is insecure, he may have no skills, he has no wide ramification of family connection. He is an exposed tree in a storm. Consequently he has to make sacrifices: these may be low wages, long hours, deference to authority, acceptance of poor conditions in work, food, and housing. On the average, then, a man of this type will undercut the more expensive native, who has his roots further in. Consequently it is probable that one of the most marked consequences of immigration is the displacement of the native population by the newcomer. As Mr. Herbert Marshall showed, while Dominion Statistician, if there had been no immigration to Canada from the 1850's and if the country had kept its natural increase, it would have come out with as large a population as it then had. It is to be questioned whether immigration, except under special conditions, really increases population at all.

Canada's population, as I have said, has grown in three hundred years from a few hundred to eighteen millions. One of the largest constituents in it, the French, has grown without aid of immigration. The rest of us are or will be just as thorough mongrels as the French are thorough breds. There are people in the country from every land under the sun. In time, they will come together, though this process has not yet gone far. The term *Canadian* yesterday meant a person either of French or British descent. Tomorrow it will mean a person either of French or a dozen other descents. A new people forms slowly. It is forming under our eyes, and already there are grandfathers among us who share paternity with Germans or Finns or Japanese. Not only do "breeds" mix in this way. Those qualities that "breeds" imply, far more subtle and important than the biological differences, if any, between the "breeds," they must mix also. Canada of the future no doubt will still be a country where the Anglo-Saxon public attitudes will dominate, but there will be many a home where a European breakfast is served. We are going over a road so similar to that which our American friends have already travelled that it is hard to distinguish between them. We have long ago turned our back on racial homogeneity, on the New Zealand and, until lately, the Australian policy, and have agreed to accept the risks of a non-homogeneous, a non-integral society, with every value fighting it out for survival. It is a bold experiment, perhaps a desperate one. It means national spirit or chaos: we can take our choice.

PART II: POSSIBILITIES OF COLONIZATION OF NORTHERN CANADA

INTRODUCTION

René Pomerleau, F.R.S.C.

CANADA IS ONE of the largest countries of the world but most of its population lives and thrives in a comparatively narrow strip along its southern border. The remainder is almost empty, with the exception of a few scattered oases. For a long time, only those who were searching for the Northwest Passage, or the whalers and fur traders were brave enough to travel in these hostile regions. During the last quarter of the nineteenth century the systematic exploration of the north was initiated mainly for the purpose of reaching the North Pole, but since the turn of the century these areas have been penetrated, first, to gather descriptive data, and later to obtain more basic information in a variety of scientific provinces. These efforts culminated in the last International Geophysical Year during which the exploration of the North was intensified and research activities received great support from many countries including our own.

Until a comparatively recent date, the population of Canada in general was indifferent towards the barren lands of the North and the Arctic sea, neither of which appeared to have any economic value. Now the people are aware of the political and strategic importance of the subarctic and arctic territories. The increasing needs of raw material and the population pressure in the world have also stimulated the interest and attention of governments and various agencies in these cold areas.

Although many Fellows of the Royal Society have individually contributed to the knowledge of the North and the Society itself has organized symposia which have touched certain aspects of the Arctic, particularly in oceanography, it is certainly apropos to consider the potentialities of our boreal lands as a more permanent and extensive habitat for man. Obviously we can no longer neglect such a large land and it is our duty, as a group and as individuals, to contribute to its development and to enhance its value. We should carry our share in the planning

of the future occupancy of this part of our country. Already the knowledge of northern conditions, and of the renewable and non-renewable
resources, as well as the technical advances of transportation and
living facilities, have marked such progress that it is not irrational to
think of colonizing the North. Other countries, mainly the U.S.S.R.,
are ahead of us in the actual utilization of their boreal territories. In
spite of the fact that the population pressure is less acute in Canada
than in Europe and Asia and the climate less favourable in the northwestern section of the globe, we should intensify our study of the
potentialities of the North before encouraging human penetration of
these territories.

The papers that follow, by six specialists, will help us to weigh the
future of these areas, and to appreciate the problems that should be
tackled immediately or studied more intensively.

THE RÔLE OF MINERAL RESOURCES IN THE
DEVELOPMENT AND COLONIZATION
OF NORTHERN CANADA[1]

W. Keith Buck and J. F. Henderson, F.R.S.C.

THE DEVELOPMENT AND COLONIZATION of the Canadian north will depend in the future, as in the past, mainly on the development of its non-renewable resources of metals and mineral fuels. Any forecast as to when and to what extent this development will take place must be based on the potential mineral resources of northern Canada and the demand or market for these resources to provide the incentive to search out and develop them.

Three years ago at the meeting of the Royal Society in Edmonton a symposium was held on "The Canadian Northwest: Its Potentialities." One contribution was a paper on the minerals and fuels of the Canadian Northwest which outlined in considerable detail the geology of the area, the history of mining development, present mining activities, and the possibilities of finding further deposits in a region that includes most of northern Canada.[2] In this paper we propose to deal mainly with the economic aspects of mineral development in the north. In the first part J. F. Henderson gives a general picture of the geological setting including distribution of known mineral deposits and the probable distribution of those likely to be found in the future, particularly in the less explored northern regions. In the second and more comprehensive part, W. Keith Buck discusses the resource, engineering, and economic aspects of mineral development in the north and the relation between colonization and resource development.

[1]Published by permission of the Deputy Minister, Department of Mines and Technical Surveys, Ottawa.
[2]A. H. Lang and R. J. W. Douglas, "Minerals and Fuels," in Frank H. Underhill (ed.), The Canadian Northwest: Its Potentialities (Toronto: University of Toronto Press, 1959), pp. 35–60.

PART I: GEOLOGICAL SETTING

Canada is divided into five main regions, each of which has characteristic geological features that determine the mineral potential of the provinces and territories these regions underlie. Four of the five regions extend into or lie in northern Canada. We shall discuss them in turn and the mineral deposits, known and potential, that they do or may contain.

The Canadian Shield

The Canadian Shield, forming nearly half of Canada, is saucer-like in shape sloping gently towards Hudson Bay, around which it lies only a few feet above sea-level (Fig. 1). Over most of the Shield the local relief is less than two hundred feet although in northwest Labrador and on Baffin Island mountains rise five to ten thousand feet above the sea. "Formed by the cooling of ancient heats, glaciated, eroded, granite hard, pitted by boulder beds, muskeg, beaver meadows, scribbled over by an almost indecipherable scrawl of lakes and rivers, this is the forbidding treasury from which most of Canada's mineral wealth is extorted."[3]

During the long ages of Precambrian time great accumulations of volcanic and sedimentary rocks were formed in what is now the Canadian Shield. These rocks were subjected to processes of mountain building, during which they were steeply folded and faulted, and granite and other igneous rocks formed in the roots of the mountains. These ancient mountain ranges, probably rising to thousands of feet, were worn down by erosion, the seas encroached on the resulting lowlands, and the cycle of deposition, mountain building, granite intrusion, and erosion began again. This cycle was repeated many times during the immensely long span of Precambrian time. As a result of this long and complex history the Shield now consists mainly of granite and granitoid gneisses with relatively small areas of early Precambrian strata scattered through it as isolated troughs and basins of severely deformed and altered volcanic and sedimentary rocks. These volcanic–sedimentary belts are remnants of former extensive formations that have been largely destroyed by granitization or removed by erosion. Resting on the upturned edges of these ancient volcanic and sedimentary rocks and the granitic rocks that intrude them are extensive sheets of relatively flat and undisturbed volcanic and sedimentary rocks of late Precambrian age. The Canadian

[3]Royal Commission on Canada's Economic Prospects, *Final Report* (Ottawa, 1957), p. 6.

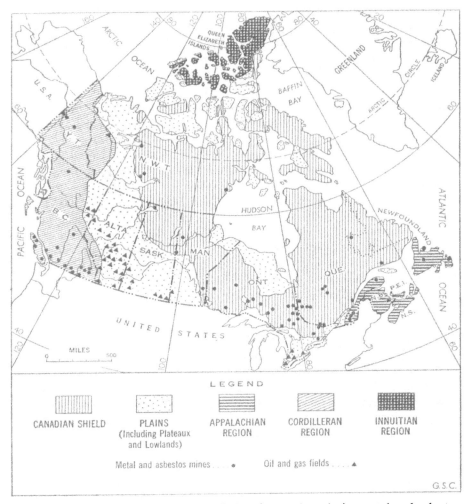

FIGURE 1. Canada, showing main geological regions and producing metal and asbestos mines, and oil and gas fields.

Shield has remained a relatively stable mass or platform since Precambrian time.

The Shield has no resources of oil, gas, or coal but the known and potential metallic mineral resources are larger than those of any of the other geological regions of Canada. About 48 per cent of Canada's total mineral production comes from it. In 1960 the Shield yielded 84 per cent of the copper, 94 per cent of the gold, 64 per cent of the iron ore, 99 per cent of the nickel, and all of the platinum and platinum group metals, uranium, and cobalt, produced in Canada. These metals were mined from the gold quartz veins of Porcupine, Kirkland Lake, and Yellowknife; the copper–zinc deposits of Rouyn-Noranda and Flin Flon, the copper–nickel–platinum deposits of the great Sudbury Basin; the iron deposits of Steep Rock Lake and the Labrador Trough; the uranium deposits of Blind River, Ontario, and Lake Athabasca; and many others.

These mines and mining camps, and in fact nearly all of Canada's producing mines in the Shield lie within 300 miles of its southern and western margins (Fig. 1). The exceptions are a small nickel–copper mine at Rankin Inlet on the west coast of Hudson Bay and the large iron mines of the Labrador Trough to which railroads have been built linking them to the coast. Other northern mines are the Eldorado uranium mine on Great Bear Lake (now closed owing to exhaustion of ore), three gold mines at or near Yellowknife on Great Slave Lake, and several uranium mines on or near Lake Athabasca all of which are relatively accessible because they are on or near the Mackenzie River system.

The concentration of producing mines along the southern fringe of the Shield is surely due to accessibility and consequently more thorough geological mapping and prospecting. Equally important, largely because the deposits are accessible, costs of exploration, development, and mining are lower in the south. Because the geological environment does not change, we have reason to expect that the distribution and abundance of ore deposits in the northern, less accessible parts of the Shield are comparable to those in the southern fringe.

The Interior Plains and Arctic Lowlands and Plateaux

The Interior Plains lie to the west of the Canadian Shield and extend north from the United States border to the Arctic Ocean (Fig. 1). Their gently rolling surface slopes imperceptibly upwards and westwards until they merge with the Foothills of the Rocky Mountains. To the north and northeast, the Arctic Islands Lowlands and Plateaux are the northeasterly continuation of the Interior Plains. For the most part they are rolling lowlands or plains sloping gradually to the sea but over large areas, particularly in the eastern part, sea cliffs rise abruptly 500 to 1500 feet to deeply incised plateau-like surfaces which attain still greater elevations inland.

The Interior Plains are underlain by strata that range in age from

Cambrian to Early Tertiary. They include sandstones, shales, limestones, and dolomites that are nearly flat-lying and undisturbed. Most of the beds formed in seas of moderate to shallow depth but some of the younger deposits accumulated in fresh or brackish water. Probably some of the Palaeozoic and Mesozoic strata once extended over large areas of the Shield but have been worn away by erosion.

The most important known mineral resources of the Interior Plains are oil, natural gas, and coal; other characteristic deposits include potash and common salts and gypsum. Bituminous sands of Lower Cretaceous age outcrop for 118 miles along the Athabasca River in the Fort McMurray area of Alberta and form a great reserve from which petroleum and other products may some day be obtained. And millions of tons of lead–zinc ore have been found in Middle Devonian dolomite near Pine Point on the south shore of Great Slave Lake.

The Interior Plains of Central Alberta, northern British Columbia, Saskatchewan, and Manitoba contain the largest known oil and gas fields in Canada. The value of crude petroleum and natural gas produced in 1960 from this region amounted to about 19 per cent of Canada's total mineral production. About 21 per cent of Canada's coal came from the same region, nearly all of it south of Edmonton. Almost all of our oil, gas, and coal mines are concentrated in the southern part of the Interior Plains, mainly south of a line drawn between Fort St. John and Edmonton (Fig. 1). Similar favourable geological conditions for the accumulation of oil and gas prevail in northern Alberta, British Columbia, and the Northwest Territories north to the Arctic Ocean. And beyond, in the Arctic Islands Lowlands and Plateaux, several sedimentary basins containing 10,000 feet or more strata offer promise.[4] We may reasonably assume that the potential mineral fuel resources of these large unexplored areas compare favourably with those of the more thoroughly explored and productive southern part of the Interior Plains. Moreover, the possibility of finding lead–zinc ore bodies in the far north, similar to those southwest of Great Slave Lake, should not be overlooked.

Cordilleran Region

The Cordilleran Region includes all the mountain-built or disturbed strata, including the Foothills, west of the Interior Plains. It extends

[4]A. F. Gregory, Margaret E. Bower, and L. W. Morley, "Geological Interpretation of Aeromagnetic Profiles from the Canadian Arctic Archipelago," and R. Thorsteinsson and E. T. Tozer, "Summary Account of Structural History of Canadian Archipelago since Precambrian Time," in Gilbert O. Raasch (ed.), *Geology of the Arctic* (Toronto: University of Toronto Press, 1961), pp. 427–37, 339–60.

from the United States border throughout the length of British Columbia, part of Alberta, all of the Yukon, and part of the Northwest Territories (Fig. 1). The higher peaks rise to 12,000 feet and, in the St. Elias Mountains of northern British Columbia and the Yukon, Mount Logan reaches nearly 20,000 feet.

The Cordilleran Region is on the site of a great basin of sedimentation where seas and fresh-water basins existed during much of the time from Late Precambrian to Late Mesozoic and Early Tertiary. The mountains of the Western Cordillera are carved in a complex of sedimentary, volcanic, and granitic rocks. Great thicknesses of sedimentary strata with interbedded volcanic rocks ranging in age from Late Precambrian to Early Mesozoic have been folded, faulted, and intruded by granitic rocks of several ages, mainly in the Mesozoic era. The mountains so formed have been eroded to expose the granitic cores over large areas, and the mineral deposits associated with them. The Western Cordillera contains a wide variety of metallic mineral deposits including in particular silver, lead, zinc, and copper, but also mercury, iron, tungsten, and gold. And in northern British Columbia asbestos in ultrabasic intrusions has been discovered comparatively recently and is being mined. Of Canada's mineral production in 1960 the Western Cordillera produced 48 per cent of the silver, 85 per cent of the lead, and 8 per cent of the asbestos.

The mountains of the Eastern Cordillera were formed from a great thickness of sedimentary strata ranging from Late Precambrian to Tertiary in age. Sedimentation continued long after the strata of the Western Cordillera were folded and mountain-built. The Eastern Cordillera, although highly folded and faulted, has not undergone sufficient erosion to expose the deep-seated granitic rocks that doubtless form its roots or the metallic mineral deposits associated with them. But along its eastern foothills geological conditions have been favourable for the development of important accumulations of natural gas and oil, and deposits of coal. In the Foothills of southern Alberta, oil and natural gas have been developed in four major fields. Far to the north in the Mackenzie River valley, is the Norman Wells oilfield and in the northern Yukon, in the Peel River Plateau, a deep exploratory well has penetrated an oil- and gas-bearing zone.

Although the Cordillera extends from the United States' border to the Arctic Ocean, nearly all the producing mines are within 250 miles of the border or near the accessible coast (Fig. 1). To the north, producing mines are limited to the Cassiar asbestos mine in northern British Columbia near the Yukon Territory, and the United Keno silver–lead–zinc mine in central Yukon Territory, and gold placer deposits of the Klondike—both accessible because on the navigable Yukon River system. As in Canada's other geological regions, the concentration of mines in the south is due to the greater attention the more accessible areas have received. The geological environment of the Northern Cordillera is equally favourable; potential mineral resources in metals and oil and gas are probably equally large. Recent developments such as those near Stewart in northern British Columbia where 26 million tons of good grade copper ore have been indicated, in the southwestern Yukon where large deposits of tungsten have been discovered, and on the Peel River Plateau in the northern Yukon where an exploratory well has tapped a zone containing oil and gas, all give promise that this is so.

Innuitian Region

The Innuitian Region of the northerly Arctic Islands is underlain, in the main, by moderately to intensely folded sedimentary rocks ranging in age from Precambrian to Tertiary. Just as the unfolded or gently flexed strata of the southern Interior Plains of Alberta pass to the west into the folded structures of the Cordillera, so the undisturbed strata of the Arctic Islands and Plateaux pass to the north into the folded structures of the Innuitian Region—a belt up to 200 miles wide with peaks rising to 10,000 feet in the northern part of Ellesmere Island (Fig. 1).

Of particular economic interest are the Parry Islands and Cornwallis Islands fold belts to the north of the Arctic Plains and Plateaux, and still farther north, the large Sverdrup sedimentary basin containing more than 40,000 feet of Palaeozoic, Mesozoic, and Tertiary strata.[5] These large areas of moderately folded rocks are favourable both stratigraphically and structurally for the accumulation of oil and gas and have marked similarities to other regions of the world producing large quantities of petroleum.[6] Exploration of the Innuitian Region has hardly begun but, though expensive, should be rewarding.

Conclusions

Although northern Canada may be well endowed with potential mineral resources, it does not necessarily follow that these resources

[5]Thorsteinsson and Tozer, "Summary Account of Structural History of Canadian Arctic Archipelago since Precambrian Time."

[6]Y. O. Fortier, A. H. McNair, and R. Thorsteinsson, "Geological Petroleum Possibilities in Canadian Arctic Islands," Amer. Assoc. Pet. Geol., Bull. no. 10, 38 (1954), 2075–109. A. Bryce Cameron, "Queen Elizabeth Islands of Arctic Canada and their Petroleum Prospects," J. Inst. Pet., 47, 449 (1961), 129–61.

will be found and exploited. Canada has no monopoly on the world's mineral deposits, and other nations and continents, notably Asia, Africa, and South America, have potential resources comparable to our own. The present problems of the Canadian mining and petroleum industries are largely problems of marketing and export rather than production and supply. These may persist and in the future, in increasing degree, the Canadian mineral industry must adjust to a rapidly changing pattern of world trade as the less developed nations with great potential mineral resources enter the world market. As our mineral industry moves north, costs of exploration, development, and exploitation rise. Ultimately, the major question is if our potential mineral resources buried in the wind-swept barren lands of the north and the snowy wastes of the Arctic Archipelago can be exploited to compete with those of more hospitable lands.

PART II: RESOURCE, ENGINEERING, AND ECONOMIC ASPECTS

The Place of the Mineral Industry in the Economy of the Yukon and the Northwest Territories

In contrast to Part I, the term "Northern Canada" shall here denote only the Yukon and the Northwest Territories, a valid restriction because of political rather than geographical or physiographic boundaries. Under the British North America Act, natural resources, including minerals, come within the jurisdiction of the respective provinces. In the case of the two territories mentioned above, the federal government has a provincial responsibility for resources and it is its policies which directly affect the development of resources rather than those of the provinces to the south or east. On the national level, of course, policies of the federal government can, and do, have a marked indirect effect on the development of resources throughout the whole of Canada.

Mention has been made in Part I of the distribution of mineral deposits known at present. It would seem logical, at this point, to describe and analyse the actual mining operations which are now in existence. Firstly, it is important to describe the place which mineral production holds in the total economy of the Yukon and the Northwest Territories. It will be seen from an examination of Table I, that mining in 1958 accounted for 83.2 per cent of the net value of commodity production in the two territories, dwarfing the economic contributions of all other forms of industrial activity. Electric power, the second most valuable industry at 6.2 per cent of the net value of commodity production, is in large part produced by a Crown corpora-

TABLE I

NET VALUE OF COMMODITY PRODUCTION BY INDUSTRY, YUKON AND THE NORTHWEST TERRITORIES, 1954-8

	1954		1955		1956		1957		1958	
	Thousands of dollars	Per cent	Thousands of dollars	Per cent	Thousands of dollars	Per cent	Thousands of dollars	Per cent	Thousands of dollars	Per cent
Agriculture	—	—	—	—	—	—	—	—	—	—
Forestry	595	1.5	449	1.2	1,152	3.6	625	2.1	952	3.0
Fisheries	636	1.7	742	2.0	787	2.4	720	2.4	682	2.2
Trapping	939	2.5	1,410	3.8	961	3.0	842	2.8	854	2.7
Mining	32,516	85.8	31,098	84.3	26,543	82.5	25,014	82.2	26,163	83.2
Electric power	1,364	3.6	1,462	4.0	1,660	5.2	1,807	5.9	1,951	6.2
Manufactures	1,856	4.9	1,733	4.7	1,076	3.3	1,410	4.6	859	2.7
Construction	—	—	—	—	—	—	—	—	—	—
Total	37,906	100.0	36,894	100.0	32,179	100.0	30,417	100.0	31,461	100.0

Source: Statistics Section, Mineral Resources Division, Department of Mines and Technical Surveys; compiled from D.B.S. statistical reports.

TABLE II

PRINCIPAL MINERAL INDUSTRY STATISTICS, YUKON AND THE
NORTHWEST TERRITORIES, 1930–59

	Number of establishments	Number of employees	Salaries and wages (in dollars)	Cost of fuel and electricity and process supplies (in dollars)	Net value added (in dollars)
1959					
Yukon	58	764	3,634,914	3,682,200	7,486,433
N.W.T.	86	1,180	6,717,354	5,908,630	20,493,199
Total	144	1,944	10,352,268	9,590,830	27,979,632
1958					
Yukon	55	723	4,097,107	2,383,655	6,673,258
N.W.T.	80	1,203	6,862,291	4,026,194	19,490,095
Total	135	1,926	10,959,398	6,409,849	26,163,353
1950					
Yukon	22	604	2,586,281	1,786,502	7,597,298
N.W.T.	80	884	3,249,770	1,645,321	6,377,212
Total	102	1,488	5,836,051	3,431,823	13,974,510
1940					
Yukon	11	617	1,518,747	695,692	3,091,943
N.W.T.	16	441	880,414	623,965	1,539,206
Total	27	1,058	2,399,161	1,319,657	4,631,149
1930					
Yukon	24	319	835,525	90,834	2,583,481
N.W.T.			Not available		
Total	24	319	835,525	90,834	2,583,481

Source: Statistics Section, Mineral Resources Division, Department of Mines and Technical Surveys; compiled from D.B.S. statistical reports.

tion. In contrast, mineral industry development in the Territories has been undertaken largely by private industry.

That mineral resources are important to the North has been succinctly expressed by Mr. R. G. Robertson, Deputy Minister of Northern Affairs and National Resources, in a recent statement: "I think it safe to say that no substantial economic development is likely to be based on renewable resources . . . nothing based on the renewable resources of the north, with the sole exception of hydro-electric power can ever be sufficient in scale to form a substantial economic base or to provide an important addition to the national income of Canada. . . . I think it is clear to anyone who makes a serious study of the northern part of this country . . . that the interesting prospects depend on the non-renewable resources: on mining and on oil and gas."[7]

[7] R. G. Robertson, "The North: Its Problems and Its Possibilities," an address to the Canadian Club, Ottawa, February 17, 1961.

TABLE III

MINERAL PRODUCTION, YUKON AND THE NORTHWEST TERRITORIES, 1925–60

Year	Yukon (thousands of dollars)	N.W.T. (thousands of dollars)	Total: Yukon and N.W.T. (thousands of dollars)	Total: Canada (thousands of dollars)	Per cent: Yukon of Canada	Per cent: N.W.T. of Canada	Per cent: Yukon and N.W.T. of Canada
1960	12,180	23,633	35,813	2,476,240	0.5	0.9	1.4
1959	12,592	25,874	38,466	2,409,020	0.5	1.1	1.6
1958	12,311	24,895	37,206	2,100,739	0.6	1.2	1.8
1957	14,112	21,401	35,513	2,190,322	0.6	1.0	1.6
1956	15,656	22,158	37,814	2,084,906	0.7	1.1	1.8
1955	14,725	25,598	40,323	1,795,311	0.8	1.4	2.2
1954	16,589	26,414	43,003	1,488,382	1.1	1.8	2.9
1953	14,739	10,300	25,039	1,336,303	1.1	0.8	1.9
1952	11,386	8,945	20,331	1,285,342	0.9	0.7	1.6
1951	9,793	8,289	18,082	1,245,483	0.8	0.7	1.5
1950	9,036	8,051	17,087	1,045,450	0.8	0.8	1.6
1945	1,239	471	1,710	498,755	0.2	0.09	0.3
1940	4,118	2,594	6,712	529,825	0.8	0.5	1.3
1935	1,302	128	1,430	312,758	0.4	0.04	0.5
1930	2,522	—	2,522	279,874	0.9	—	0.9
1925	1,792	—	1,792	226,583	0.8	—	0.8

Source: Statistics Section, Mineral Resources Division, Department of Mines and Technical Surveys; compiled from D.B.S. statistical reports.

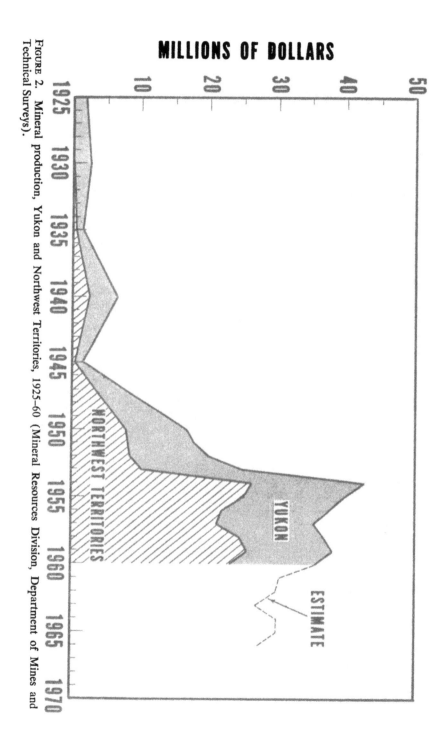

FIGURE 2. Mineral production, Yukon and Northwest Territories, 1925–60 (Mineral Resources Division, Department of Mines and Technical Surveys).

TABLE IV

Expenditure on Prospecting by Metal Mining Companies, Yukon and the Northwest Territories, 1950-59

Year	Yukon (in dollars)	N.W.T. (in dollars)	Total: Yukon and N.W.T. (in dollars)	Total: Canada (in dollars)	Per cent: Yukon of Canada	Per cent: N.W.T. of Canada	Per cent: Yukon and N.W.T. of Canada	Per cent: Prospecting Expenditure Yukon and N.W.T. of value of mineral production Yukon and N.W.T.	Per cent: Prospecting Expenditure all Canada of value of mineral production of Canada
1959	272,212	1,335,346	1,607,558	43,017,635	0.6	3.1	3.7	4.2	1.8
1958	464,656	1,428,619	1,893,275	32,507,086	1.4	4.4	5.8	5.1	1.5
1957	783,838	2,818,007	3,601,845	54,424,419	1.4	5.2	6.6	10.1	2.5
1956	1,735,608	1,395,388	3,130,996	48,400,259	3.6	2.9	6.5	8.3	2.3
1955	1,609,040	756,349	2,365,389	26,928,541	6.0	2.8	8.8	5.9	1.5
1954	1,757,422	354,922	2,112,344	26,815,235	6.6	1.3	7.9	4.9	1.8
1953	328,400	1,394,831	1,723,231	17,832,758	1.9	7.8	9.7	6.9	1.3
1952	536,578	1,743,538	2,280,116	13,578,174	4.0	12.8	16.8	11.2	1.1
1951	174,282	198,466	372,748	9,176,439	1.9	2.2	4.1	2.1	0.7
1950	134,115	87,361	221,476	5,353,267	2.5	1.6	4.1	1.3	0.05

Source: Statistics Section, Mineral Resources Division, Department of Mines and Technical Surveys; compiled from D.B.S. statistical reports.

The value of mineral production in the Yukon and the Northwest Territories in 1960 amounted to about thirty-six million dollars, 1.4 per cent of the total value of mineral production of all Canada. In both absolute and relative terms, the share which the two territories have of Canadian mineral production has been declining since the peak year of 1954 (see Table III and Fig. 2). The outlook for the immediate future is that of further decline, again in both absolute and relative terms. The decline which has and probably will continue to take place has occurred despite the relatively large expenditures on exploration in the two territories compared with the relatively small value of mineral production in the territories and compared with the exploration expenditures in all Canada (see Table IV). In 1959, the most recent year for which statistics are available, Yukon and the Northwest Territories accounted for 3.7 per cent of the total Canadian expenditure on metal mining exploration. For the same year, exploration expenditure in the two territories amounted to 4.2 per cent of the total value of the mineral production of the territories; in comparison, the total expenditures for metal mining exploration in all Canada amounted to 1.8 per cent of the total value of Canadian mineral production, indicating very clearly the relatively large amount of effort devoted to mineral exploration in the territories, in comparison with the probable return on the exploration dollar expended (see Table IV).

Minerals Now in Production

There are now five companies operating lode mines, one company producing oil, and one company producing coal in the two territories (see Table V), from which gold, silver, lead, zinc, nickel, copper, cadmium, coal, natural gas, and crude petroleum are obtained. Although all are naturally of local importance, only those mines producing silver and gold make any significant contribution to Canadian mineral production; in 1960, the Yukon produced 20.9 per cent of all silver produced in Canada and the two territories combined produced 10.6 per cent of Canada's entire output of gold (see Table VI).

Gold.[8]   Gold was the first mineral to be produced in what are now the two territories. There are probably few Canadians who do not respond to the tales of the Yukon Gold Rush and the romance of the timeless search for gold, so well commemorated in the poems and

[8]The information in this section is based on material given in T. W. Verity, "The Canadian Gold Mining Industry in 1960," Mineral Information Bulletin, Mineral Resources Division, Department of Mines and Technical Surveys, Ottawa (in preparation).

TABLE V

Producing Mining and Oil Companies, Yukon and the Northwest Territories, 1961

Company	Mine	Location	Minerals	Size	Year production commenced
Metal mines					
United Keno Hill Mines Limited	Elsa Hector Calumet Galkeno	*Yukon* Mayo Area Keno Hill	silver lead zinc cadmium	500 t/d	Feb. 1947
North Rankin Nickel Mines Limited		*N.W.T.* Rankin Inlet	nickel copper	250 t/d	June 1957
Giant Yellowknife Mines Limited		*N.W.T.* Yellowknife	gold	1,000 t/d	May 1948
The Consolidated Mining and Smelting Company of Canada Limited	Con and Rycon	*N.W.T.* Yellowknife	gold	500 t/d	July 1938
Consolidated Discovery Yellowknife Mines Limited		*N.W.T.* Giauque Lake	gold	150 t/d	Jan. 1950
Placer gold mines					
Action Mining Company	Bullion Creek	*Yukon* Kluane Lake	gold	1,806 oz/yr	Jan. 1923
The Yukon Consolidated Gold Corporation Limited	Bonanza Creek Hunker Creek Dominion Creek Sulphur Creek	Dawson	gold	53,516 oz/yr	(year amalgamation of several small producers)
Yukon Explorations Limited	Five Finger Creek Glacier Creek	Sixty Mile	gold	1,794 oz/yr	1946
Ballarat Mines Limited	Groetcher Hill Dominion Bench	Dawson	gold	5,687 oz/yr	
The Burwash Mining Company Limited	Burwash Creek	Kluane Lake	gold	953 oz/yr	

18 other operators produced in excess of 50 troy ounces each of gold in 1960.

Company	Mine	Location	Minerals	Size	Year production commenced
Coal mines					
Yukon Coal Company, Limited	Tantalus Butte	*Yukon* Carmacks	Coal	4,000 t/yr	1900
Oil wells					
Imperial Oil Limited		*N.W.T.* Norman Wells	oil	1,350 bbl/day	1921

Source: Information and Special Projects Section, Mineral Resources Division, Department of Mines and Technical Surveys.

TA▮

VALUE OF INDIVIDUAL MINE▮
NORTHWEST TERRITO▮

	Gold (in dollars)	Silver (in dollars)	Lead (in dollars)	Zinc (in dollars)	Nickel (in dollars)	Cop (in do▮
1960						
Yukon	2,638,736	6,011,779	1,873,919	1,377,216	—	▮
N.W.T.	13,961,924	64,904	—	—	3,200,000	3▮
Total	16,600,660	6,076,683	1,873,919	1,377,216	3,200,000	3▮
Total Canada	156,171,715	28,726,788	40,427,281	108,209,749	312,738,234	264,3▮
Per cent Yukon and						
N.W.T. of Canada	10.6	21.2	4.6	1.3	1.0	▮
1955						
Yukon	2,492,379	5,037,035	3,774,575	2,978,881	—	▮
N.W.T.	11,092,001	51,565	—	—	—	▮
Total	13,584,380	5,088,600	3,774,575	2,978,881	—	▮
Total Canada	156,788,528	24,676,472	58,314,500	118,306,466	215,866,007	239,7▮
Per cent Yukon and						
N.W.T. of Canada	8.7	20.6	6.5	2.5	—	▮
1950						
Yukon	3,551,549	2,588,486	1,861,957	861,873	—	▮
N.W.T.	7,635,227	50,198	—	—	—	▮
Total	11,186,776	2,638,684	1,861,957	861,873	—	▮
Total Canada	168,988,687	18,767,561	47,886,452	98,040,145	112,104,685	123,2▮
Per cent Yukon and						
N.W.T. of Canada	6.6	14.1	3.9	0.9	—	▮
1945						
Yukon	1,221,258	11,824	5,976	—	—	▮
N.W.T.	333,218	956	—	—	—	▮
Total	1,554,476	12,780	5,976	—	—	▮
Total Canada	103,823,990	6,083,166	17,349,723	33,308,556	61,982,133	59,32▮
Per cent Yukon and						
N.W.T. of Canada	1.5	0.2	0.03	—	—	▮
1940						
Yukon	3,097,633	864,176	156,524	—	—	▮
N.W.T.	2,123,621	22,760	—	—	—	▮
Total	5,221,254	886,936	156,524	—	—	▮
Total Canada	204,479,083	9,116,172	15,863,605	14,463,624	59,822,591	65,77▮
Per cent Yukon and						
N.W.T. of Canada	2.6	9.7	1.0	—	—	▮

*Operation suspended September 1960.
N.A. not available.
Source: Statistics Section, Mineral Resources Division, Department of Mines and Technical Surveys; compiled▮
from D.B.S. statistical reports.

ꝒUCED, YUKON AND THE
–60

anium (dollars)	Cadmium (in dollars)	Colum-bium (in dollars)	Tanta-lum (in dollars)	Cobalt (in dollars)	Coal (in dollars)	Natural Gas (in dollars)	Crude petroleum (in dollars)	Total (in dollars)
—	203,788	—	—	—	74,414	—	—	12,180
077,645*	—	—	—	—	—	18,000	932,000	23,633
077 645	203,788	—	—	—	74,414	18,000	932,000	35,813
335,404	3,187,591	—	—	—	76,059,631	48,027,110	432,495,700	1,733,316
1.9	6.4	—	—	—	0.1	0.04	0.2	2.1
—	360,074	—	—	—	81,806	—	—	14,725
232,079	—	1,032	9,760	16,119	—	6,213	1,185,780	25,594
232,079	360,074	1,032	9,760	16,119	81,806	6,213	1,185,780	40,319
031,604	3,262,439	1,032	9,760	8,563,700	93,579,471	15,098,508	305,640,036	1,265,895
50.8	11.0	100.0	100.0	0.2	0.09	0.04	0.4	3.2
—	130,871	—	—	—	40,960	—	—	9,036
N.A.	—	—	—	—	—	12,818	352,656	8,051
N.A.	130,871	—	—	—	40,960	12,818	352,656	17,087
N.A.	1,968,302	—	—	964,003	110,140,399	6,433,041	84,619,937	773,125
—	6.6	—	—	—	0.04	0.2	0.4	2.2
N.A.	—	—	—	—	—	—	—	1,239
N.A.	—	—	—	—	—	335	136,303	471
N.A.	—	—	—	—	—	335	136,303	1,710
N.A.	639,603	—	—	90,026	67,588,402	12,309,564	13,632,248	376,130
—	—	—	—	—	—	0.003	1.0	0.5
410,176	—	—	—	—	—	—	—	4,118
410,176	—	—	—	—	—	335	37,265	2,594
410,176	—	—	—	—	—	335	37,265	6,712
410,176	1,056,152	—	—	1,235,220	54,675,844	13,000,593	11,160,213	451,056
100.0	—	—	—	—	—	0.003	0.3	1.5

novels of Robert W. Service (and more recently of Pierre Berton) and so well expressed in the words:

> Over the Mountains of the Moon,
> Down the Valley of the Shadow,
> Ride, boldly ride,
> The Sage replied,
> If you seek for Eldorado.[9]

Since the discovery of gold by George Carmacks on August 14, 1896, at Bonanza Creek, placer gold production in the Yukon has amounted to 246 million dollars. To this day, placer gold mining is still carried on in the Yukon; one of the operations is on a large scale with six large dredges and one large hydraulic mine; two are large-scale hydraulic operations; and about twenty-five are small placer operations. All are in receipt of financial assistance under the Emergency Gold Mining Assistance Act. Placer gold production is now in the order of 2.6 million dollars a year and it amounts to 1.7 per cent of total Canadian gold production. The largest operator, Yukon Consolidated Gold Corporation Limited, accounts for 67 per cent of all placer gold production.

In the Northwest Territories substantial gold production comes from four mines operated by three companies: Giant Yellowknife Mines Limited; the Con and Rycon mines of The Consolidated Mining and Smelting Company of Canada Limited, all near the town of Yellowknife, and Consolidated Discovery Yellowknife Mines Limited, some sixty-five air miles north of Yellowknife. The latter mine is the highest grade gold mine in Canada, with a value per ton of gold and silver from four to ten times as great as the large gold mines farther south in Ontario and Quebec. However, its costs per ton are also from three to five times as great as those same mines. The other three mines are also among the highest grade gold mines in Canada with gold and silver values from two to three times greater than the large gold mines in Ontario and Quebec and costs three to five times greater. Giant Yellowknife, the largest producer, is now Canada's third largest lode gold mine.

None of these mines is now in receipt of financial assistance as provided by the Emergency Gold Mining Assistance Act. Exploration and development are carried on continuously at all four mines and ore reserves have been maintained at a relatively constant level for several years. Lode gold production in the Northwest Territories amounts to

[9]Anon.

8.9 per cent of the value of total Canadian gold production and 60 per cent of the value of all the mineral production of the Northwest Territories (1960).

Silver. Virtually all (99 per cent) of the silver production in the two territories comes from the mines of United Keno Hill Mines Limited in the Mayo area of the Yukon. Although these mines also produce lead, zinc, and some cadmium, the ore contains an average of about thirty-eight ounces of silver per ton. The mines are more properly termed silver mines and are Canada's largest single source of silver. In 1960, United Keno Hill produced 20.5 per cent of the entire Canadian output of silver. It is the second most important mineral produced in the territories, following gold, and it accounts for 16.8 per cent of the entire mineral production of the territories. Its value to United Keno Hill is almost double that of lead and zinc. In addition to the silver produced by United Keno Hill, minor amounts are produced as a by-product from the lode gold mines in the Northwest Territories.

The presence of rich silver-lead ore in the Mayo District became known about 1906, but owing to its remoteness there was little production until about 1921. Except for the period from 1942 to 1947, production has been almost continuous. Ore reserves at the end of September 1960 totalled 512,577 tons averaging 38.39 ounces of silver, 6.36 per cent lead, and 4.84 per cent zinc.

Lead and Zinc.[10] In addition to silver, United Keno Hill Mines Limited has an important production of lead and zinc amounting, respectively, to 4.6 and 1.3 per cent of Canada's total output. The output from the mines, in the form of lead and zinc concentrates and silver precipitate, is shipped via Whitehorse, Skagway, and Vancouver to the smelter of The Consolidated Mining and Smelting Company of Canada Limited at Trail, British Columbia. Transportation is by truck to Whitehorse, rail to Skagway, boat to Vancouver, and rail to Trail.

Cadmium. Although the production of cadmium from the mines of United Keno Hill Mines Limited is relatively small in value, it still amounts to 6.4 per cent of Canada's total output of cadmium. The metal is recovered from the lead and zinc concentrates at the Trail smelter of The Consolidated Mining and Smelting Company of Canada Limited.

---

[10]The information in this section is based on material given in D. B. Fraser, "A Survey of the Primary Zinc Industry in Canada, 1959," Mineral Information Bulletin MR 43, Mineral Resources Division, Department of Mines and Technical Surveys, Ottawa.

Nickel and Copper. In mid-1957, North Rankin Nickel Mines Limited brought into production a nickel-copper mine located at Rankin Inlet on the west coast of Hudson Bay. In 1960 the output from this mine amounted to 1 per cent of Canada's total production of nickel. Copper production is small, amounting to one-third of a million dollars in 1960. At the end of October 1960, ore reserves, amounting to 177,120 tons, grading 3.47 per cent nickel and 0.99 per cent copper, were sufficient for two more years of operation at the current operating rate. For some time the company has been actively exploring the nearby area for new deposits; in the summer of 1961 it had parties in the field in an area ninety miles to the south of the mine. The output from the mine has been shipped for treatment by rail from Churchill to the Fort Saskatchewan refinery of Sherritt Gordon Mines Limited.

Coal. At Carmacks, Yukon Territory, a small amount of coal has been produced intermittently since 1900 from an underground mine employing less than a dozen persons; production currently amounts to 0.1 per cent of Canada's total output of coal.

Petroleum and Natural Gas.[11] The Norman Wells oilfield supplies an important part of the oil requirements of western sections of the Northwest Territories. The field, a Devonian reef, was discovered in 1920 from oil seeps noticed in the area. It operated intermittently until World War II, when field capacity was expanded to supply military installations in Alaska; the field has been in continuous operation since 1944. Production from the field amounts to 1.2 per cent of the Canadian total output of crude petroleum. The field is small and it is producing at much below its productive capacity. A minor amount of natural gas is produced in association with the oil at Norman Wells. At present, the principal destination of the oil is Yellowknife, by water transportation up the Mackenzie River.

Major Mineral Deposits with Production Potential

Lead and Zinc.[12] The operating mines and the Norman Wells oilfield, although of some local importance, have little significance in the total Canadian production of minerals. Other mineral deposits are known which show some possibility of development, the largest of which is the major zinc-lead deposit of The Consolidated Mining and Smelting Company of Canada Limited, located at Pine Point on the

[11]R. A. Simpson, "A Survey of the Petroleum Industry in Canada 1959," Mineral Resources Information Bulletin MR 48 Mineral Resources Division, Department of Mines and Technical Surveys, Ottawa.

[12]The information in this section is based on material given in Fraser, "A Survey of the Primary Zinc Industry in Canada, 1959."

south shore of Great Slave Lake. This deposit constitutes one of Canada's and the world's largest known reserves of zinc and lead.

Exploration from 1948 to 1954, combined with earlier exploration in 1929 and 1930, outlined a mineralized belt about twenty-two miles long and from two to four miles wide, containing an indicated reserve of several million tons in the shallower parts of the belt, with additional large reserves in the deeper parts. The grade of the ore was found to vary widely through the mineralized zones; large bodies were outlined averaging more than 10 per cent combined lead and zinc. The lead and zinc ratio was found to be about 1 to 4 on the average, and in the higher-grade orebodies as high as 1 to 2. The exploration programme was suspended in 1954, sufficient reserves having been proven, and no work has been done since. Further development depends on the construction of a railway to Great Slave Lake from a railhead on the Northern Alberta Railway's existing lines, which run from Edmonton to Waterways in northeast Alberta, and from Edmonton to Grimshaw in the northwest. The distance from Waterways to Pine Point is 418 miles, and from Grimshaw to Pine Point is 437 miles. On June 4, 1959, a Royal Commission was appointed "to enquire into and report upon the respective merits of the alternative routes which might be followed by a railway line to be built from northern Alberta into the southern portion of the District of Mackenzie, Northwest Territories, for the purpose of providing access to and contributing to the development of that portion of the Territories tributary to Great Slave Lake." The Commission considered a substantial number of briefs and held several days of public hearings. Following further study and analysis, it presented its report on the merits of the two routes on June 30, 1960.

In November 1960, the federal government announced its intention to conduct a survey of the western route from Grimshaw to Pine Point, as a preliminary to the construction of the railway along the Grimshaw–Pine Point route. Negotiations with the two railway companies concerned and The Consolidated Mining and Smelting Company of Canada Limited are now under way.[13] The last-named company is anxious for the commencement of construction because additional supplies of raw materials will soon be required to maintain refinery production at Trail. The principal alternative to a supply from Pine Point is the importation of zinc and lead concentrates from abroad.

For a number of years world production of lead and zinc has

[13]On June 19, 1961, notice was given in the House of Commons that a bill would be introduced to provide for the construction of a railway from Grimshaw, Alberta, to Great Slave Lake in the Northwest Territories.

exceeded consumption by substantial amounts, creating problems for world producers in the form of low prices and abnormally high inventories. Canadian and other world producers have approached these problems on an international basis, through the establishment in 1958 of a Lead and Zinc Committee, formed under the auspices of the United Nations, and in 1959 of an International Lead and Zinc Study Group which replaced the first Committee and is still functioning. It consists of twenty-five member countries, including all the principal world producers and consumers.

Believing that special remedial action would be needed, in October 1958 the United States imposed absolute quotas on imports of unmanufactured lead and zinc, designed to raise internal prices and reduce stocks of metal in the hands of United States producers, which are still in effect.

As the fifth largest world producer of lead and the second largest producer of zinc, and as a large exporter of both metals, Canada has been actively concerned in measures taken to improve the situation in world markets. Partly through the efforts of the International Lead and Zinc Study Group, but mainly through the action of natural economic forces, the situation in zinc is considerably improved today. The same cannot be said of lead, but adjustments in production and increased consumption are expected in 1961 to help in restoring a more normal balance between world production and demand.

To help maintain its important world position as a producer of zinc and lead, Canada has major deposits under development in the Mattagami area of Quebec and there are additional large reserves in the Bathurst area of New Brunswick. Total known reserves of zinc and lead in Canada amount to about 25 per cent and 19 per cent, respectively, of world reserves.

Tungsten. Canada Tungsten Mining Corporation Limited holds eighty-four unpatented mining claims just east of the Yukon-Northwest Territory boundary at about 61° 57′ latitude and 128° 16′ longitude and 135 miles north of Watson Lake. The claims cover some 4,280 acres on the west slope of Flat River valley. The discovery of the tungsten deposit was announced in 1959. During the latter part of 1959 and throughout 1960, exploration work, consisting of geological mapping, sampling of outcrop, and diamond drilling, demonstrated the existence of a tungsten deposit with indicated reserves of 1.5 million tons grading 2.4 per cent WO_3.[14] Beneficiation tests conducted in

[14]The market unit for tungsten ores and concentrates is the ton unit which is 1 per cent of a ton of tungsten trioxide(WO_3). In the United States and Canada the unit is 20 pounds of WO_3 and is called a short-ton unit (stu); in the United

Ottawa by the Mines Branch of the Department of Mines and Technical Surveys, and in Lakefield, Ontario, by Lakefield Research of Canada Limited, indicated that a commercially acceptable scheelite (Ca WO_4) concentrate could be obtained from the samples submitted.

Among the many problems that faced Canada Tungsten, once it had determined that the tungsten deposit was of a size and grade to make a mining operation attractive, were the moving of equipment and supplies into the property, the movement of concentrates out from the mine, and the finding of a market for its product. In March 1961, Canada Tungsten announced that arrangements had been made with American Metal Climax, Inc., Dome Mines Limited, and Ventures Limited to supply development capital through both a loan and a purchase of stock. In addition, Climax agreed to act as sales agent for the company's concentrates. It was also announced that the Department of Northern Affairs and National Resources would build a development road from the Ross River–Watson Lake road to Hyland Valley, a distance of eighty miles. That Department also agreed to pay two-thirds of the cost of the fifty-mile mine access road from Hyland Valley into the mine site; the company will pay the remaining one-third of the cost of the road. It is planned to complete the entire road some time in 1963, when the mine is scheduled to come into production.

Although the project is relatively small, it is of considerable importance to the Yukon and will bring Canada back into the rank of world tungsten producers. Production is planned at the rate of about 100,000 tons per year, from which it is expected to recover 200,000 units of WO_3. At present market prices ($15.75 a unit on April 27, 1961, E. & M. J.) the concentrate will have a value of about 3 million dollars. Most of the concentrate will be shipped to the United States which is deficient in tungsten resources. As Canada's imports of scheelite in 1960 were just under 38,000 units of WO_3, it is not expected that Canada Tungsten will move immediately into the Canadian market where trade patterns are well established. The capital cost of the project

Kingdom the unit is 22.4 pounds of WO_3 and is called the long-ton unit (ltu). Tungsten trioxide contains 79.31 per cent tungsten (W). Therefore, a short-ton unit contains 15.862 pounds of tungsten. Only the valuable portion of the ore is paid for and market quotations are always on this basis: that is, $20 per stu WO_3 65 per cent basis. This means that one short ton of concentrate assaying 65 per cent WO_3 would contain 65 units of WO_3 and would, therefore, be valued at 65 × 20 = $1,300. Most contracts impose a penalty for impurities. In this example, the $1,300 figure represents the price received at destination. From it must be subtracted insurance, ocean or rail shipping to destination, dock and storage charges. If a broker is handling the sale of concentrates in a particular country his commission will be about 3 per cent of the value but may, under rare circumstances, be as low as 1 per cent.

will be in the order of six million dollars; during the construction phase from 100 to 120 men will probably be employed and when the mine is in production, its operation will require about eighty men.

World production is in the order of six million short-ton units of tungsten concentrates per year (60 per cent WO_3 basis). The United States, the largest Free World consumer and importer of tungsten concentrates, is also a large producer. In 1958, consumption was some 9 million pounds of contained tungsten, of which 6½ million pounds were imported. In 1960, its consumption was the same, of which 3¼ million pounds were imported. Four countries supplied 80 per cent of United States tungsten imports in 1960; these were Portugal supplying 25 per cent, Australia, 23 per cent, Brazil, 20 per cent, and Bolivia, 12 per cent. In the United States market, Canada's chief competitors will be United States domestic producers and producers in Brazil, Bolivia, and possibly Argentina. China is the largest world producer of tungsten and it also has the largest reserves. World reserves total 174 million short-ton units of WO_3, of which 134 million are in China and 3.6 million in Canada.

Petroleum and Natural Gas.[15]   No paper on the potential resources of the two territories would be complete without some comment on the possibility of the discovery and development of petroleum and natural gas. In respect to the mainland region of the territories, there are good possibilities for the discovery of important reserves of oil and gas. Exploration has been going on for many years, particularly in the more southerly areas near the Alberta border and, more recently, near the British Columbia border, but comparatively few deep exploratory wells have been drilled. To date, in fact, exploration has been meagre.

As mentioned earlier, the Norman Wells field was discovered in 1920. In 1956 gas was discovered at Rabbit Lake, Northwest Territories, and in 1959 oil and gas were discovered in the Peel Plateau region of Yukon Territory. Since then, one or two gas discoveries have been made just north of the British Columbia border and this area, at this particular time, would seem to hold the most promise. If large reserves are found, the area immediately north of the British Columbia border would be within economic reach of the gas transmission lines leading from the Peace River area of British Columbia to the south. Other gas discoveries in northeastern British Columbia would bear part of the cost of a pipeline tapping territorial gas fields. However, much more costly exploration is required before there are

[15]The information in this section is based on material given in Simpson, "A Survey of the Petroleum Industry in Canada in 1959."

reserves large enough to warrant serious consideration of development of the area.

In spite of these widely spaced discoveries, the two territories remain relatively unexplored. However, in the realm of pure speculation, estimates have been made of the quantities of gas which might be found in the territorial mainland. One basis of speculation has been to compare the volume of sediments in Western Canada to that in highly developed gas-producing areas; the logic of this comparison is that the whole of Western Canada will produce gas in the same proportion as that produced in highly developed gas-producing areas; carrying this comparison to its ultimate conclusion, the potential gas reserves of Western Canada might be as high as 300 trillion cubic feet. On this basis, the Canadian Petroleum Association has estimated gas reserves in the territorial mainland to be 70 trillion cubic feet. Based on the fact that 6,500 cubic feet of gas were found for every barrel of recoverable oil in Canada to the end of 1960, it can further be speculated that 11 billion barrels of oil may be found associated with the potential gas reserves of 70 trillion cubic feet. In this connection, it is of interest to mention that the total reserves of oil for all of Canada to the end of 1960 are 3.7 billion barrels.

If the oil and gas resources of the territorial mainland are relatively unknown, those of the Arctic Islands are even more unknown. Recent reconnaissance geological and geophysical mapping, principally by the Geological Survey of Canada, has indicated great thicknesses of sediments and structures favourable to the accumulation of oil. However, it will require drilling to determine whether, in fact, oil and gas do occur in these sediments. To date, no major oil company has undertaken serious exploratory work in the Arctic Islands although exploration permits covering 42 million acres were issued to the end of 1960.

In 1958 Lang and Douglas analysed the situation as follows: "Some of the islands of the Arctic Archipelago are accessible by sea for only a few months of the year and those in the Northwest are, even in summer, surrounded by sea-ice. Full development of the potential fuel resources of the islands must surely await the time when the world demand for oil is such that intermittent delivery is of little consequence, or when advances in technology permit penetration of the sea-ice by shipping during the greater part of the year. The fuel resources of the islands and northerly continental region form a potential source for strategic purposes."[16] It is hoped by all Canadians that the great thickness of sediments in the Arctic Islands does harbour a large accumulation of

[16]Lang and Douglas, "Minerals and Fuels."

oil and gas and particularly the large type of oil reservoirs found in the Middle East. The existence of major oil and gas resources would seem to offer the main economic hope for the future exploitation of this most northerly part of Canada.

The two territories are relatively unexplored for oil and gas largely for economic reasons. There is a world-wide over-abundance of oil, prices have been falling, tanker rates have seldom been lower, and there would seem to be little chance of these conditions being reversed during the years immediately ahead. Oil, if found in large quantities on the territorial mainland, will meet competition from provincial production more conveniently located with respect to inland markets. That geographic location within Canada is economically important is demonstrated by the geographic advantage which Saskatchewan oil has over Alberta oil. Saskatchewan has a proportionately greater share than Alberta of markets in the United States and eastern Canada because of its greater proximity to these markets and because its shallower sediments result in lower drilling costs. The potential oilfields of the territorial mainland are far from inland markets and also from overseas markets. Well costs are exceedingly high. Sales in overseas markets would necessitate seasonal storage at some location which would permit continuous service to the market area and this, too, would be an additional cost. Another important consideration, particularly relative to the Arctic Islands, is the stake which the major oil concerns with large financial resources have in the Middle East and Venezuela. These companies must consider the return on invested capital in the Arctic Islands compared with capital invested in other areas of the world or even compared with that invested in Western Canada.

Iron.[17] Large deposits of iron-bearing material are known to occur on the Belcher and Nastapoka islands in Hudson Bay. The iron deposits on Belcher Islands were investigated by Belcher Mining Corporation Limited between 1953 and 1957. Exposures near Haig Inlet on Flaherty Island have been known for many years; they consist principally of fine-grained, banded, siliceous, iron-bearing material in which the iron occurs as varying mixtures of hematite and magnetite. Diamond drilling has indicated a large tonnage of material grading in excess of 40 per cent natural iron. Twenty claims and two fractions in the Haig Inlet area are subleased from Belcher Island Iron Mines Limited on a

[17]The information in this section is based on material given in R. B. Elver, "A Survey of the Iron Ore Industry in Canada in 1959," Mineral Resources Information Bulletin MR 45, Mineral Resources Division, Department of Mines and Technical Surveys, Ottawa.

royalty basis. The balance of the properties held by the company in the area was acquired by staking. No work has been done on the property since 1957.

On Nastapoka Islands, iron-bearing formations were first discovered some eighty years ago. Sporadic exploration and examination has continued since their discovery. The mineralization consists essentially of extremely fine-grained siliceous jasper containing minute grains of silica coated with red iron oxide. The jasper occurs in thin, broken bands with the partings filled with a finely divided mixture of hematite jasper and some magnetite. Preliminary mineral dressing studies on samples of the iron-bearing material have indicated that it would be difficult to effect a good separation and obtain high enough recoveries yielding a product of commercial grade.

On the coast of Hudson Bay, in Quebec, to the east and southeast of Belcher Islands, there are iron deposits of considerable size at Duncan Lake and Great Whale River. Although these are outside the two territories, they are mentioned because of their apparent mineralogical and economic superiority over the iron deposits on the Belcher and Nastapoka islands. However, all these deposits must be considered in relation to the total situation in iron ore—both in Canada and in the world. There is no global shortage of iron ore although there are regional shortages. Canada itself possesses tremendous resources of iron ore, more favourably situated in comparison with the territorial deposits, in Quebec–Labrador and in Ontario immediately north of the Great Lakes. There are three possible markets available for the Hudson Bay deposits: the Great Lakes iron and steel centres in the United States and Canada, the east coast centres in the United States, and the European market.

It is a peculiarity of the North American iron and steel industry that producers of iron ore are traditionally affiliated with producers of iron and steel either through association with established marketing agents or through direct financial participation by the major steel companies. Thus an independent ore producer would have a difficult time selling his product in the United States or Canadian market unless some corporate affiliation had been arranged. When considering the Great Lakes market the following factors must be taken into account: the short shipping season on Hudson Bay which would require adequate docking, loading, shipping, and storage facilities to enable the movement of large tonnages; high freight costs owing to the distance to be travelled and the number of trans-shipments required; the difficulty of market penetration; and competition from established and proposed producers in that portion of Ontario lying just north of the Great Lakes. These latter companies have the advantages of short communication lines over routes already established, ready availability of supplies and labour, and corporate integration with large Canadian and United States iron and steel producing firms.

It would appear, then, that the most promising market for the Hudson Bay iron ores would be in Europe and that the development of this market would depend on the ability of the mines to land a suitable product at European ports at a suitable price, in competition with year-round shipments from Quebec–Labrador and from South America, Africa, and northern Europe. Undoubtedly, the handicaps imposed by this competition and by Canadian geography are tremendous.

Other Minerals. Some description has been given and some analysis made of the possible future production in the Territories of lead and zinc, petroleum and natural gas, iron ore and tungsten—the first three because of the presence or possible presence of large resources; the last because a tungsten mine is now being developed. These, of course, are not the only known occurrences of minerals in the two territories. Indeed, there are innumerable occurrences of minerals in diverse geological environments: occurrences of base metals, lead, zinc, copper and nickel; of the precious metals, gold and silver; and of iron.[18] There are also known occurrences of other minerals such as asbestos, columbium and tantalum, beryllium, uranium, gypsum, and coal. However, except for the gold deposit at Taurcanis, none of these occurrences has yet proven of a size and grade to warrant serious underground exploration for ore.

The Market

Some comment has already been made about the Canadian and world markets in respect to lead and zinc, petroleum, tungsten, and iron ore. There will be a world surplus in petroleum for a number of years and this surplus will continue to affect Canadian production and marketing. There is a world abundance of iron ore and Canada will face increasing competition in world markets in the years ahead. It is com-

[18]J. C. McGlynn, "Mineral Potential of the Northwest Territories," paper presented at the Western Annual Meeting of the Canadian Institute of Mining and Metallurgy, Vancouver, October 1960; W. R. A. Barager, "The Mineral Industry of the Precambrian Shield District of Mackenzie: Present and Future," paper presented at the 25th Annual Meeting of the Alberta and Northwest Chamber of Mines and Resources, Edmonton, January 13, 1961; W. R. A. Barager, "The Mineral Industry of the District of Mackenzie, Northwest Territories," Paper 61–3, Geological Survey of Canada, Department of Mines and Technical Surveys (Ottawa, 1961).

mon knowledge that there is a world surplus of uranium and a great lack of commercial markets, a situation which is expected to continue for a number of years. The price of gold has remained the same for twenty-five years, thereby discouraging the exploration for and development of gold deposits. Both the short-term and the long-term market for Canadian silver look promising because world consumption exceeds annual world production by substantial amounts. Although it may take time, it should be possible to develop a market for Canadian tungsten because the United States lacks it.

It is not possible in this paper to analyse in detail the present and future Canadian and world markets for all minerals which are or might be produced in the two territories. However, some comment over and above that made on the preceding pages would seem to be warranted in respect to the non-ferrous metals. It will be recalled that the Royal Commission on Canada's Economic Prospects made the following forecast of Canadian consumption for the years 1965 and 1980.[19]

	1955	1965	1980
	(thousands of short tons)		
Nickel	4	10	15
Copper	139	165	225
Zinc	58	70	100
Lead	66	75	90

Events since these forecasts were made have brought about certain changes in consumption and in 1960 consumption was, in thousands of short tons:

Nickel	5
Copper	117.6
Zinc	55.8
Lead	40.2

Here is a situation where, midway between the base year 1955 and 1965, the first year forecasted, consumption of three of the four metals was lower than that of the base year and consumption of the fourth metal, though higher, was still far short of the forecast.

Canada has lagged far behind in the growth of consumption of the major non-ferrous metals (see Table VII). It will be noted that in 1950 Canada consumed 2.9 per cent of total world consumption of these metals whereas in 1959 Canada consumed only 2.2 per cent. In contrast, it is interesting to note the growth of consumption in the European

[19]John Davis, "Mining and Mineral Processing in Canada," Royal Commission on Canada's Economic Prospects (October, 1957).

TABLE VII

WORLD CONSUMPTION OF NON-FERROUS METALS, 1950 AND 1959
(THOUSANDS OF METRIC TONS)

	World total	EEC	EFTA	USA	Canada	Soviet sphere
1950						
Aluminum	1,583.6	162.1	228.8	823.0	59.1	244.3
Lead	1,878.3	307.5	321.2	803.0	49.6	190.0
Copper (refined)	3,009.3	441.6	512.8	1,292.2	97.0	399.1
Zinc	2,075.0	360.0	293.0	915.0	49.3	248.0
Tin	170.3	24.3	27.9	72.3	4.6	17.0
Nickel	158.2	12.4	20.4	90.7	2.9	30.0
Total	8,874.7	1,307.9	1,404.1	3,996.2	262.5	1,128.4
Per cent of World Total		14.7	15.8	45.0	2.9	12.7
1959						
Aluminum	3,988.6	540.1	418.5	1,846.1	80.4	790.0
Lead	2,378.3	493.3	364.7	609.3	44.8	540.0
Copper (refined)	4,341.1	867.9	636.6	1,311.6	117.9	828.0
Zinc	2,880.6	629.5	330.7	831.4	59.9	590.0
Tin	184.5	33.9	32.5	46.2	4.3	32.2
Nickel	246.7	33.9	33.4	102.2	4.0	59.0
Total	14,019.8	2,598.6	1,816.4	4,746.8	311.3	2,839.2
Per cent of World Total		18.5	13.0	33.9	2.2	20.3
Per cent increase over 1950	58.0	98.7	29.4	18.8	18.6	151.6

Compiled in Mineral Resources Division, Department of Mines and Technical Surveys, from statistical yearbooks of *Metallgesellschaft* and *Minerais et Métaux*.

Economic Community (EEC) and in the Communist nations, as portrayed in Table VII.

In March 1960, Mr. Simon D. Strauss, a world marketing authority on lead and zinc, predicted that by 1970 consumption of lead in the United States would be 15 per cent greater than in 1960, and 20 per cent greater in the rest of the free world—or average increases of 1.5 per cent and 2.4 per cent annually. He also estimated a 15 per cent growth in zinc consumption in the United States and 25 per cent elsewhere.

Sir Ronald Prain, on October 11, 1960, in an address before the Rhodesian Economic Society, stated that the recent growth in consumption of refined copper in the free world has averaged 4.4 per cent per annum and that, barring a general world recession, a slightly higher rate of 4.6 per cent can be expected until approximately 1965, after which it is anticipated it will decline to 4 per cent by 1980.

Nickel consumption in the free world rose to a new high in 1960 and was about 20 per cent over the previous record established in 1959, and about double the annual rate in the years immediately preceding the Korean War. The Paley Report predicted a requirement of 264,000 tons in 1975; in 1960, consumption at 258,000 tons was already close to this level and there is every indication that the market for nickel will continue to increase in the period between now and 1975.

Canadian trade in non-ferrous metals will tend to be more and more with Europe, notwithstanding certain impediments created by the tariff policy of the European Economic Community. The less developed nations will also provide outlets for metal if these markets are sought and developed by Canadian producers.

In a recent paper dealing with the development of northern mineral resources W. S. Kirkpatrick, President of the Consolidated Mining and Smelting Company of Canada Limited, emphasized repeatedly the dependence of northern mineral development on export markets, stating that: "the objective behind Northern development must, in the final analysis, be purely economic, that is, having the Northland contribute to our national wealth by using its raw materials to produce goods which can be sold to advantage . . . Northern development will not be for the purpose of providing goods for the domestic market. It will have to be for the purpose of producing basic commodities for export . . . . the rate at which resources of Canada's Northland can and will be exploited depends, in the final analysis, on our ability to expand our export trade."[20]

In a more general way, the dependence of northern mineral development on market demand was summed up well by Lang and Douglas: "We consider that, excepting occasional spectacular finds, increase in the production of minerals will depend mainly on increase in national or international demands. The greatest uncertainty seems therefore to be not in the ultimate potential but in the rate of growth of the demands."[21]

Economic and Engineering Considerations

The engineering considerations of import to northern development have been brilliantly described by Robert F. Legget.[22] Similarly, the economic considerations of import to northern mineral development have been

[20]W. S. Kirkpatrick, "Challenges and Opportunities in Developing Canada's Northland," paper presented at the 25th Annual General Meeting of the Alberta and Northwest Chamber of Mines and Resources, Edmonton, January 13, 1961.

[21]Lang and Douglas, "Minerals and Fuels."

[22]Robert F. Legget, "An Engineering Assessment," *in* Underhill (ed.), *The Canadian Northwest: Its Potentialities.*

analysed in detail by the writer's Division and are well described in one of its publications.[23] This paper draws liberally from that publication.

The problems inherent in mining in Canada's northern regions are varied and difficult to assess from an economic viewpoint. Costs are dependent on geographical factors, size of operation, type of extraction process required, availability of labour, and company policy concerning labour and inventories. Many factors tend to increase these costs over those for mining operations in more southerly parts of Canada. In Dubnie's study, an attempt was made to arrive at a "cost increment for northern operations" which was defined as "the additional cost to a northern mining company of an item compared to the cost of that item in the more southerly parts of Canada." In this investigation it was found that the cost increment can be added to the cost of transportation, power, services to employees, heating, supply inventory, and capital investment.

Transportation. There is general agreement that the cost of transportation is the greatest single deterrent to the development of northern mineral resources. The cost of transportation affects exploration costs by increasing the amount of money required to maintain parties in the field; it affects production costs by raising the cost of incoming equipment and supplies and reducing the net return on outgoing mine products; and it affects living costs for all personnel in the area. Terrain presents transportation problems independent of distance. Most of the North is covered with muskeg and underlain by permafrost, both of which add greatly to the costs of road construction and maintenance. Permafrost hinders the gathering of gravel (a scarce material in much of the North) for road construction because only relatively thin layers can be scraped off between periods of thawing. Permafrost under muskeg or in poorly drained, waterlogged silt makes a poor road base; when the thawed portion (active layer) is broken by vehicles, an impassable waterlogged surface soon results.

It is understandable that the operating mines in the Northwest Territories are so located that they can take advantage of comparatively low cost, albeit seasonal, water transportation. The pioneer methods of transportation—by barge over the navigable Athabasca, Slave, and Mackenzie rivers or by ocean-going ship into Hudson Bay—are the major means of supplying established producers. Rates by water trans-

---

[23]Amil Dubnie, "Some Economic Factors Affecting Northern Mineral Development in Canada," Mineral Information Bulletin MR 38, Mineral Resources Division, Department of Mines and Technical Surveys (Ottawa, December 1959).

port are lower than for any other existing form of transportation but the shipping season is restricted. It varies from two to five months along the Athabasca–Slave–Mackenzie system, depending on the location of the producer. In Hudson Bay, the season is two-and-one-half months from late July to early October; it is, in effect, determined by the normal insurance period for ocean-going ships. Insurance rates for shipping in Hudson Bay are high, being about $2.00 per ton for iron ore.

The importance of aircraft in the development of the north cannot be over-emphasized. Most of the present northern producers owe their discovery to this mode of transportation. Exploration programmes now in progress rely almost entirely on aircraft, and supplies and equipment for preliminary development are also transported chiefly by this means. In the Northwest Territories the abundance of lakes provides convenient landing strips for exploration aircraft. Established producers use air transport for supplying operations with perishables, for moving personnel, and for shipping out high-value products.

Railroads are virtually non-existent, there being only the White Pass and Yukon Railway with fifty-eight miles of rail north of the British Columbia border to Whitehorse in the Yukon. Roads are few and in the Northwest Territories are confined to connecting links between Yellowknife, Fort Providence, Hay River, and the Mackenzie Highway. Construction has barely started on a road running northeasterly from Yellowknife. In the Yukon, the road system consists essentially of the Alaska Highway to Whitehorse with connections southwards to the northern part of British Columbia and north and northeasterly to Dawson City, Keno Hill, and Fairbanks. Construction has commenced on a road from Watson Lake to Ross River. The federal government, through its Department of Northern Affairs and National Resources, has increased somewhat the tempo of road construction in the two territories with a view to encouraging further mineral exploration and development and to improving connections with the southwesterly part of Canada. Although the programme is, of necessity, costly and slow, it has the positive effect of adding materially to the sparse road network already in existence.

The cost increment resulting from the higher cost of transportation in the northern part of Canada compared to the more southerly parts is considered to be a minimum of $1.00 a ton mined, being the increased transportation cost for a mine located at Yellowknife compared to a mine located at Edmonton, the closest major supply base, although it, too, is still 2,000 miles from major markets.

Power. Power, whether supplied by diesel or hydroelectric installations is more expensive in the north and the cost increment would again amount to about $1.00 a ton mined. The Yukon is far more abundantly supplied with potential hydroelectric resources than the Northwest Territories but in every instance water power development depends on the economic justification provided by the mineral resource. A large mining operation or a closely grouped number of small mining operations might justify the installation of a large hydroelectric plant and attendant transmission lines. Construction of a plant to serve an isolated producer could hardly be justified unless the location and size of the required plant were ideal and the projected life of the mining operation long enough to amortize the plant and attendant installations. At United Keno Hill Mines, for instance, the company must bear the whole cost of a power plant and thirty miles of transmission lines, amortized over a twenty-one-year period; the cost is high compared to the cost of power from diesel generators at other territorial mining operations. Of the costs for local diesel power, the largest single item, often amounting to 80 per cent, is fuel. If land or water transportation is not available, the cost of diesel fuel alone could use up much of the returns from mining operations. A choice would have to be made between high-cost diesel power or hydroelectric power from distant plants. This problem alone can prevent exploitation of small deposits unless the ore tenor is unusually high. The economics of packaged nuclear power plants have yet to be proven.

Labour. Maintenance of adequate labour in a northern location is one of the major problems facing northern operators. Numerous methods are employed to attract and hold labour, from outright transportation allowances and company-sponsored shopping facilities to less obvious subsidies on housing, messing, bonus earnings, and recreational facilities. Burdens of education and hospitalization costs are normally carried initially by the companies until communities are established and then governments provide assistance. Turnover of northern labour varies generally between 50 and 200 per cent per year, but there appears to be a relation between the type of labour employed and the turnover. Mines which make a practice of hiring inexperienced men and constantly promoting their own employees appear to enjoy the lowest turnover. Other factors which appear to be critical are quality of food for single personnel, housing cost to married personnel, and quality of recreational facilities. Several mining companies operate general stores where employees purchase at cost. Prices in such stores compare favourably with those prevailing in large cities.

Summer recreational facilities are relatively easy to provide owing to the presence of numerous lakes and rivers in the north which have excellent facilities for boating and fishing. Swimming is possible in many locations but short summers and cool waters tend to limit it. One mine north of Yellowknife provides an outdoor heated swimming pool for the use of its employees. Activities not associated with bodies of water, such as hunting, are possible, but the discomforts associated with an unbelievably large insect population must be experienced to be appreciated. Winter activities such as curling, bowling, and other indoor sports are possible. Provision of facilities for these activities is generally sponsored by the producing companies who must bear the major portion of the cost. Local leadership in the use of facilities is seldom lacking. Despite provisions for winter recreation, morale during the long winter sinks, as shown by monthly turnover records which indicate a peak turnover in early spring.

Hourly rates do not differ substantially from those prevailing in established mining camps elsewhere but contract rates are generally higher and the occupations covered by contracts include many of the "service" occupations. Cost increments owing to transportation allowances can easily be evaluated, as all companies keep accurate records of such payments. Use of Eskimo labour eliminates costly transportation charges normally accruing from use of transient white men but present experience with Eskimo labour—perhaps based on the Eskimo attitude towards the accumulation of wealth—shows considerable absenteeism and loss of efficiency. Other qualities of the Eskimo, such as cheerfulness and acceptance of authority, offer promise for the future when Eskimos become accustomed to regular employment.

Large-scale operations appear to be more economic with regard to labour cost increments. Overhead on messing, housing, heating, and related items appears to be considerably lower per unit of production. Turnover is lower in large communities which have a wider variety of interests to offer than isolated operations. Employees are usually hired on term contracts, generally of one year duration, with both transportation in and transportation out paid by the company, subject to completion of the contract.

Monetary outlays for labour by northern operators vary considerably, depending on management policy. The average for a group of representative mines, where reasonably complete records were available, amounts to $0.70 per ton mined. This figure includes subsidies for labour transportation, for boarding, married housing, heating, and recreational facilities. Adding to this an increment for bonus payments and bearing in mind that loss of efficiency owing to turnover cannot be evaluated, a labour increment of $1.00 per ton mined should be approximate.

It appears that maximum opportunity for reduction of labour fringe costs exists in conducting operations on as large a scale as possible, on careful selection and promoting of labour to reduce turnover, on provision of superior quality food and accommodation for single personnel and the lowest possible cost of living for married personnel. These factors are believed to be listed in the approximate order of importance.

Heating. It is perhaps obvious that fuel and heating costs are higher in northern areas than in more southerly areas and a comparison of the annual degree-days of heating required at certain locations is proof of the obvious. The cost increment for this item amounts to about $0.25 per ton mined, hardly comparable to the cost increments for transportation, power, or labour, but most likely to remain as a permanent fixture on the northern cost sheets. The estimate does not include the additional capital costs which are incurred for insulated surface boxes housing service lines, or capital expenditures for additional heating and related equipment such as boilers and oil storage tanks. As failure of a northern heating system would be a major catastrophe, systems are generally designed to be as "fool-proof" as possible.

Capital Costs. For a given capacity, capital investment on mining plant and camp facilities will be greater than that required in the south because skilled labour and building materials must be brought in from "outside" at high transportation costs. Permafrost and muskeg will be responsible for further increments resulting from construction of permanent facilities. Cost of providing winterized temporary and permanent housing and recreational facilities must not be minimized. In the Arctic, construction of surface buildings during the winter is unusually difficult. Temperatures as low as —40°F, accompanied by 40-mph winds, were common on one project while the foundations for a concentrate storage building were being poured. Performance of skilled tradesmen at $3.00 per hour was only a fraction as efficient as that normally achieved elsewhere.

The main economic determinant in civilian design is the high cost of skilled labour and materials; the answer, in part, lies in prefabrication where possible. A well-known eastern Canadian construction company that has had considerable experience in northern construction estimates that the cost of building a plant in a northern environment is about 40 per cent greater than that for a comparable plant in large eastern centres. Major increases in cost are attributable to transportation charges, provision of adequate facilities for labour, increased cost of material owing to modified designs for northern climate, and tie-up of capital for a longer construction period. All these suggest a cost increment of about $1.00 per ton mined, an estimate about equal in magnitude to that for transportation, power, and labour.

Inventories. Cost increments on money invested in stores and supply inventory are related to transportation facilities as well as to physical distance, and, to a lesser degree, to company policy. Such costs of northern operation are often overlooked in general assessments, but they constitute a continuing and significant cost for the mine operator. In many locations in the two territories, supplies are replenished on an annual basis; heavy items of equipment probably are replenished annually in most locations.

Although some recovery processes depend on large quantities of one commodity, such as sulphur, the money invested in inventory is considerably higher for the northern operator who must build up supplies annually. At northern operations the greatest portion of the inventory is in mill reagents and fuel, followed by appreciable investment in machine parts and mine supplies. From a comparison of the inventories at a number of northern operations, it appears that a fair increment figure could vary from $0.25 to $1.00 per ton mined, depending on the location of the producer and type of process, and it could possibly average $0.50 per ton mined. This amount represents the interest on the extra capital investment needed to maintain large inventories.

Base metal producers in a northern location are faced with special problems in respect to inventory of concentrates. Producers of low-bulk high-value products are not faced with comparable problems because their products can be flown out with minimum delay and at relatively low cost. Interest on the value of concentrate inventory represents an appreciable cost to base metal mines, however.

Summary of Incremental Costs. Adding together the incremental costs for transportation, power, labour, heating, capital, and inventories, the total additional cost inherent in many operations conducted in northern Canada amounts to about $4.75 per ton mined. Although this is a high figure, it could in certain instances be higher. In the final analysis, its level is dependent upon factors which, in large part, arise out of geography and climate.

From a review of the current northern operations described earlier in this paper, it is apparent that a mineral deposit must be of an unusually high grade to absorb the increased costs of northern operation. The three lode gold mines in the Yellowknife area, the silver–lead mines in the Keno Hill area, and the nickel mine at North Rankin Inlet, all owe their existence as mining operations to the high mineral values in their ores. The high tungsten values in the Flat Creek ore deposits make possible the development of this mine. Another feature common to profitable mining operations in the two territories is the economic advantage in the production of a high-value, low-bulk concentrate. Obviously mining operations such as those producing precious metals and uranium have greater potentiality than those producing base metals which require extensive transportation facilities. Most industrial minerals fall in the latter category as they are usually of such bulk in relation to value that their use is confined largely to centres of population and industry in close proximity to their source.

Incentives to Mineral Exploration and Development

National. At the beginning of Part II, it was pointed out that the provinces hold jurisdiction over mineral resources and that in the two territories the federal government has a responsibility similar to that of the provinces and also that national policies of the federal government can have a marked indirect effect on the development of resources throughout the whole of Canada. In its national rôle, the federal government provides incentives to the mineral industry surpassing by far those to other Canadian industries and comparable to those of any other country in the world. The effect on the national economy and the development of the hinterlands of Canada is obvious to the most casual of observers.[24]

Virtually every mile of railroad built in Canada since the end of World War II has been the direct result of mineral development. Excluding Pacific Great Eastern Railway extensions, which were only partially based on minerals, new rail construction to mineral developments has amounted to 1,326 miles. The Mattagami and the proposed Pine Point rail lines will add another 500 miles of rail construction. But not only is the mineral industry important to new rail construction; about 43 per cent (1959) of *all* revenue freight traffic carried in Canada consists of primary mine products. The figure rises to well over 50 per cent if one includes mineral products in all stages of manufacture.

Minerals and products of the mineral-based industries are becoming of even greater importance in Canada's export trade. The value of such exports exceeds the value of exports of any other industry and in 1960

[24]W. Keith Buck, "The Canadian Mineral Industry—At Home and Abroad," Mineral Information Bulletin MR 49, Preliminary Survey of the Canadian Mineral Industry in 1960, Mineral Resources Division, Department of Mines and Technical Surveys (Ottawa, 1961).

accounted for 31.8 per cent at the unprocessed and semi-processed level, and 41.6 per cent including fully manufactured mineral products. The value of exports of mineral and mineral products increased by 124 per cent from 1950 whereas the value of all exports increased by only 40 per cent during the same period.

One of the incentives which has contributed much to the growing rôle of the mineral industry in the Canadian economy is the three-year period of tax exemption for new mines; this is a benefit unique to the mineral industry.[25] Another substantial benefit is that which permits mineral enterprises to deduct from their taxable income all exploration, drilling, and development expenses incurred in the search for petroleum, natural gas, or minerals in Canada; in the case of a new mining enterprise these expenses may be deducted following the three-year tax-exempt period, thereby extending the tax-exempt period for a number of months or years depending on the scale of the enterprise. A third major benefit is the 33⅓ per cent depletion allowance granted in perpetuity to mineral enterprises to compensate for the exhaustion of the natural resource. There are a number of additional miscellaneous benefits such as generous depreciation allowances under certain conditions and customs duty and sales tax concessions; however, these additional benefits, although substantial, are of lesser importance than the first three described above. In many instances, mineral enterprises become substantial tax contributors; in 1958, for instance, nearly 20 per cent of all federal income taxes declared by companies and corporations came from companies engaged in the production of basic minerals and in the manufacturing and fabricating of mineral products. However, under certain circumstances, some mineral enterprises never pay corporate income taxes.

All these benefits are available to mineral enterprises in the two territories as well as to mineral enterprises elsewhere in Canada. In an effort to encourage northern development, the federal government, through its Department of Northern Affairs and National Resources, provides additional assistance over and above that normally extended in the various provinces. In the case of the Yukon tungsten development, governmental assistance in various forms will amount to approximately three-and-one-half million dollars; capital investment by the company itself will amount to about six million dollars. With an annual production

[25]E. C. Hodgson, "Summary Review of Federal Taxation and Certain Other Legislation Affecting Mining, Oil and Natural Gas Enterprises in Canada," *Mineral Information Bulletin* MR 42, Mineral Resources Division, Department of Mines and Technical Surveys (Ottawa, 1961).

valued at about three million dollars and with such benefits as the three-year period of tax exemption, preproduction write-offs, and depletion allowance, it will be many years before the enterprise contributes to the national treasury through the payment of corporate income taxes. The benefits which the enterprise will bring to the national economy are of a different kind. It will open up a new part of the Yukon and it will be of some assistance in improving our adverse balance of trade with the United States.

The example of the Yukon tungsten development is given in order to indicate the amount of assistance required to make certain mineral developments economic in terms of the developing and benefiting company, short of the government undertaking mineral development itself. An example of a different order is the proposed lead and zinc mine at Pine Point; here capital investment will be in the order of twenty million dollars, excluding eighty-five million dollars for the construction of a railway. Unlike all other mineral developments in other parts of Canada during the past fifteen to twenty years this project will be feasible only if the government provides a large part of the money required to construct and operate the railroad—again a penalty imposed by the geographic location of the property. Valuable as benefits under the Income Tax Act are, further assistance is frequently required in order to obtain mineral development in the two territories.

Territorial. Turning now to the rôle of the federal government in the implementation of its provincial responsibilities in the two territories, the greatest area of its influence on mineral exploration and development is through its mineral regulations. In this area, it is in direct competition with every other province in an endeavour to attract exploration and development capital. Provincial—and territorial—mineral regulations, no less than national policies, can induce or hinder exploration and development capital, as many examples throughout Canada and the world illustrate. In view of the geographic and economic handicaps to exploration and development in the two territories, the provisions of its mining regulations must offer greater than normal inducements if companies are to be persuaded to undertake exploration or development programmes in the north. In an endeavour to provide such encouragement, the territorial regulations on mineral exploration and development have recently been revised, but it is too early to assess the success of these changes.

Colonization and Resource Development

A reference was made earlier to the high rate of turnover in northern mining operations, which obviously affects colonization. The majority of the staff and employees of northern mining enterprises never regard the North as their permanent home. They are on "temporary appointments" of a few months' or, occasionally, a few years' duration. This feeling is so genuine and so widespread that it is, in many instances, recognized in formal contracts for term employment. Of course, the very nature of the industry has conditioned persons to the concept that a mining camp, particularly one in the hinterlands, is a place of temporary employment. Non-renewable resources must inevitably become depleted, in real or economic terms, or both. When this occurs, a ghost town results unless a renewable resource or some form of industrial activity is available. In the two territories the presence of renewable resources is almost entirely lacking, certainly in the quantities sufficient to provide stability to mining communities.

On the Norwegian island of Spitsbergen in the Arctic Ocean there are deposits of coal which have been mined for some years but there is no permanent population; miners are, in fact, employed on short-term contracts and are attracted by special tax benefits. In the Northwest Territories itself, a flourishing uranium mine operated at Port Radium on the shore of Great Bear Lake for a period of about twenty-three years. The mine was closed down in September 1960 upon the exhaustion of its ore reserves. Between 1933 and 1939 and between 1942 and 1960 an active community existed at Port Radium; in 1961 it was a ghost town. At Sherman Lake, in the Marian River area 100 miles northwest of Yellowknife, a small uranium mine and community existed for two years from 1957 to 1959. Upon the exhaustion of the ore reserves the mine was closed down and the plant and equipment were sold. In this instance, almost nothing remains. At North Rankin Inlet on the west coast of Hudson Bay there has been a small mining community in existence for three-and-one-half years. The proven ore reserves will be exhausted within two years and, with its exhaustion, unless the company is able to locate more ore, this mining community probably will also become a ghost town. This will create no unusual problem for the white miners who are accustomed to the "come and go" of mining enterprises, but the situation may be different for the Eskimos who have been trained to the white man's way of life. There is no nearby mine requiring the services of a trained indigenous mining crew. Yet the fate of mining enterprises and their supporting communities is no different in the northern part of Canada from the fate of those farther south. For instance, a large mine and community existed at Sherridon in west central Manitoba in the years from 1930 to 1951 inclusive. At one time the mine employed about 550 persons and the community contained about 200 householders and some 240 school children. The exhaustion of ore reserves

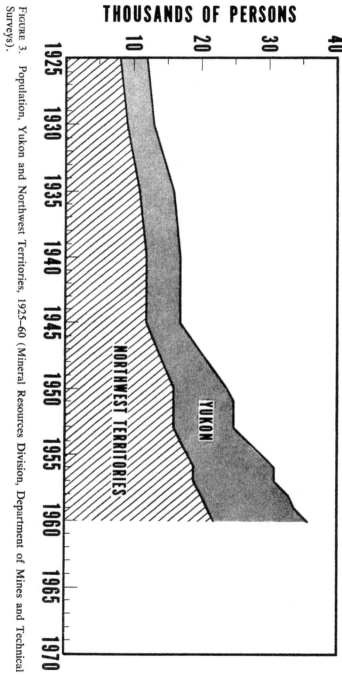

FIGURE 3. Population, Yukon and Northwest Territories, 1925–60 (Mineral Resources Division, Department of Mines and Technical Surveys).

in 1951 meant the virtual end of the community. Some capital was saved, however, by the mass movement of homes and some larger buildings over the snow to a new mine site 172 miles to the north.

Similarly, the existence of certain other communities in the two territories depends on the life of the supporting mineral deposits. A possible exception may be Yellowknife which has become, to some extent, a supply centre for the western part of the Northwest Territories. However, much of Yellowknife is dependent upon the nearby lode gold mines. Farther south lies the mining community of Beaverlodge on the north shore of Lake Athabasca. By the end of 1960 only two producing uranium mines remained and their sales contracts have only about three more years to run. The effect of further possible mine closures on Beaverlodge and the adjacent company towns may provide some useful lessons for Yellowknife.

The very nature of mineral deposition makes the development of mining enterprises an unsatisfactory and certainly temporary means of colonization. In fact, it does not provide a means of colonization in the true sense of the word. Such mining communities as have attained a semblance of permanency have usually had renewable resources, or circumstances permitting other forms of industrial activity, or the mineral resource has been of a grade, size, and geographic location to make possible the growth of a large smelting enterprise. The possibilities of any of these three circumstances existing in the northern part of Canada are not great.

Robert F. Legget assessed the situation in the following words:

It will, therefore, require strong economic incentives to produce any major increase in population in the Northwest and this can arise only from mineral development, since public expenditure *per capita* already far exceeds that for anywhere else in Canada. And mineral development is usually a strictly economic proposition. If the Northwest can produce minerals that can compete, in the markets of the world, with minerals produced elsewhere after allowing for all transportation costs, the Northwest may advance rapidly; if not, then advance must be slower. Anyone who has seen, as I have, buildings being hauled miles to be used in a new town—buildings from the town of Goldfields on Lake Athabasca, founded in the thirties but abandoned and deserted in the early fifties—cannot forget the sensitivity to external factors that will govern the development of the Northwest, just as long as mineral exploitation has to be the basis of its economy.

I believe in the future of the North, and particularly in the certain future of the Northwest. I am, however, very conscious of the difficulties, both physical and economic, that lie in the way of its development. I do not share in a literal sense the optimism of the writer who said, of the North, that "the resources are great enough to overcome the problems." The time scale to which development will take place is surely the only aspect of the North upon which there can be understandable difference of opinion.[26]

All this is not to say that the population of the North will not grow; it has indeed grown steadily, albeit slowly, since 1925 (see Table VIII) and in 1960 it numbered 36,000 persons. The lesson to be learned, if indeed there is a lesson, is that mineral development must be undertaken as a source of supply for domestic or foreign mineral markets, and not as a means of colonization. To believe that colonization and mineral resource development go hand-in-hand is to deny the facts of mineral occurrence and depletion.

TABLE VIII

POPULATION, YUKON AND THE NORTHWEST TERRITORIES, 1925-60

	Yukon (in thousands)	N.W.T. (in thousands)	Total (in thousands)	Canada (in thousands)	Per cent Yukon and N.W.T. of Canada
1960	14	22	36	17,814	.20
1959	13	21	34	17,442	.19
1958	13	20	33	17,048	.19
1957	12	19	31	16,589	.186
1956	12	19	31	16,081	.193
1955	11	18	29	15,698	.184
1954	10	17	27	15,287	.177
1953	9	16	25	14,845	.168
1952	9	16	25	14,459	.173
1951	9	16	25	14,009	.178
1950	8	16	24	13,712	.175
1945	5	12	17	12,072	.141
1940	5	12	17	11,381	.149
1935	5	11	16	10,845	.147
1930	4	9	13	10,208	.127
1925	4	8	12	9,294	.129

Source: Statistics Section, Mineral Resources Division, Department of Mines and Technical Surveys, Ottawa; compiled from D.B.S. statistics.

That mineral development in northern Canada is necessary and desirable for its own sake is certainly true. The first essential for future development is basic knowledge of the geological and mineralogical environment of the two territories, now being acquired by the Department of Mines and Technical Surveys under an accelerated programme. The use to which this knowledge is put will depend on the encouragement and incentives given to exploration and development by both federal and territorial governments, on the economic factors in northern

[26]Legget, "An Engineering Assessment," *in* Underhill (ed.), *The Canadian Northwest: Its Potentialities,* pp. 21–2.

exploration and development, and on the markets which exist for the resultant mineral products.[27]

[27]Other references on this subject include: H. S. Bostock, "Potential Mineral Resources of Yukon Territory," Paper 50-14, Geological Survey of Canada, Department of Mines and Technical Surveys (Ottawa, 1950, reprinted 1954) and "Yukon Territory—Selected Field Reports of the Geological Survey of Canada, 1898–1933," Memoir 284, Geological Survey of Canada, Department of Mines and Technical Surveys (Ottawa, 1957); K. H. J. Clarke, "The Position of the Canadian Non-Ferrous Mineral Industry in the World Economy," paper presented at the Annual General Meeting of the Canadian Institute of Mining and Metallurgy, Quebec City, March 1961; F. H. Collins, "The Yukon Territory," brief presented to the Royal Commission on Canada's Economic Prospects by the Commission of the Yukon Territory at Edmonton, Alberta, November 22, 1955; Geological Survey of Canada, *Geology and Economic Minerals of Canada* (4th ed., Econ. Geol. Ser. No. 1, 1957); W. B. Hunter, "Water Transportation Mackenzie River Watershed," paper presented at the Annual General Meeting of the Canadian Institute of Mining and Metallurgy, Quebec City, March 1961; C. S. Lord, "Mineral Industry of District of Mackenzie, Northwest Territories," Memoir 261, Geological Survey of Canada, Department of Mines and Technical Surveys (Ottawa, 1951); W. D. C. Mackenzie, "Review of Petroleum and Natural Gas in the North," paper presented at the 25th Annual General Meeting of the Alberta and Northwest Chamber of Mines and Resources at Edmonton, January 13, 1961, *Western Miner and Oil Review* (May 1961), pp. 28–33; N. L. Nicholson, "The Northwest Territories—Geographical Aspects," *Can. Geog. J.* (January 1960); Hardy Nielsen, "Economic and Physical Factors and the Arctic Future," *Oil in Canada* (February 23, 1961); R. G. Robertson, "The Northwest Territories —Its Economic Aspects," brief presented to the Royal Commission on Canada's Economic Prospects by the Commission of the Northwest Territories at Edmonton, Alberta, November 22, 1955; and "The Canadian Mineral Industry in 1960," Mineral Resources Division, Department of Mines and Technical Surveys, Ottawa (in preparation).

POSSIBILITIES OF LIGHT AND HEAT FROM
ATOMIC ENERGY AND OTHER SOURCES

E. W. Humphrys

APART FROM TECHNICAL CONSIDERATIONS, which must not be minimized, the possibility of light and heat, or power, in the general sense, being derived from atomic or nuclear energy is a question of economics as compared with conventional sources of energy, i.e., fossil fuels and hydroelectric power. The present appeal of the use of atomic energy for northern communities is based on the fact that the problem of fuel supply would virtually be eliminated and consequently fuel costs would be minimized. In northern Canada the major sources of energy for light, heat, and power currently are oil and hydroelectric power. Oil is generally supplied in the form of light fuel oil, frequently identified as Arctic Diesel Oil, but where conditions are suitable various grades of heavier and hence cheaper oil are being used successfully.

The Norman Wells oilfield, situated as it is on the Mackenzie River approximately midway between Great Slave Lake and the Arctic Ocean and accessible to a well-developed system of marine transport, provides the western portion of the Northwest Territories with an adequate supply of petroleum products at a considerable saving in cost as compared with supply from southern sources. However, the short shipping season of only three to four months on this inland waterway results in low annual utilization of transport facilities; this factor and the great distances involved create transport costs of considerable magnitude. Consequently, products priced at six to eighteen cents per gallon at Norman Wells have a delivered cost, assuming bulk transport, ranging from fourteen to thirty-five cents per gallon, to which must be added storage and inventory costs involved in providing a twelve-month supply. For locations where bulk shipment by tanker barge is impracticable, delivery by drums can result in costs approaching seventy-five cents per gallon or upwards of $1.00 if air transport is involved.

Oil supply for the eastern part of the North and the Yukon is from southern sources but costs fall within the same range. We may, therefore, conclude that the use of oil as a source of energy in the North involves a basic fuel cost ranging from eighty-five cents to approximately $2.00 per million BTU's of energy where bulk transport is available, and up to $6.00 per millon where transport costs are excessive. Translated into electrical and space-heating terms these figures indicate a fuel cost ranging from one to seven cents per kilowatt hour, and, assuming a burning efficiency of 70 per cent, from $1.60 to $7.00 per million BTU's of heating. With additions to cover capital, operating, and maintenance costs, indications are that the cost of electricity from oil may range from three to ten cents per kilowatt hour, exclusive of distribution costs.

In some areas of the North electricity can be economically produced by the development of hydro power; consequently there are at present seven separate hydro plants, ranging in capacity from a few hundred up to 15,000 horsepower, operating in the Yukon and the Northwest Territories, not to mention several major hydro developments on the northern fringes of the provinces. With hydro power, the basic fuel cost is virtually nil, if water-right charges are ignored, but capital costs are substantial and vary greatly with the location and size of the development. However, in the Northwest Territories and the Yukon we find that the wholesale cost of hydro power delivered in bulk to industrial consumers or supplied to urban distribution systems for resale, ranges from approximately 1.0 to 2.6 cents per kilowatt hour, including main transmission from the generating plant to the load centre, but not local distribution costs. If used for space-heating this would represent an energy cost ranging from approximately $3.00 to $8.00 per million BTU's; in other words, the equating price of oil would be from approximately thirty-five to ninety cents per gallon. All the hydro power developed to date in the Northwest Territories and the Yukon is in areas where oil is available at costs ranging from sixteen to forty or fifty cents per gallon and, in general, the higher cost hydro is coincident with the higher cost oil; thus, there are currently no sites where hydro power can be considered competitive with oil for heating purposes. There are exceptions where surplus capacity, which may be of a more or less temporary nature, permits the supply of secondary or withdrawable power at special rates designed to be competitive with the local cost of oil. However, generally speaking, it is improbable that firm hydro power can be developed in the North for less than one cent per kilowatt hour.

As previously mentioned, the use of atomic energy seems attractive because of the difficulties of fuel supply and cost. At present, in the absence of actual operating experience we have to rely upon estimates by competent authorities which indicate that the basic cost of nuclear fuel as supplied to a plant might vary from as low as thirteen-and-a-half cents up to approximately $2.50 per million BTU's, depending upon the type and size of the development. Thus, it is apparent that while there is considerable scope for atomic energy in the north, there are areas where competition from conventional sources would be severe as far as fuel costs are concerned. There is, however, the advantage that the fuel charge for a nuclear plant is comparatively small physically, and hence may be transported by air at reasonable cost per unit of energy. Also, a single fuel charge may last for several months or even years. Indeed, it is in the realm of logistics, attendant upon the problem of fuel supply, that atomic energy may well have its greatest appeal in connection with the more remote sites, regardless of economic considerations.

These highly attractive features of atomic power are not in themselves sufficient to establish a definite place for atomic energy in the North, in its present state of development. The methods of utilizing atomic energy for power and space-heating are still being developed. Although great strides have been made in the development of large-scale projects only a comparatively small amount of work has been done on plants of a size that are likely to be of interest for the North. In the United States work is proceeding on a number of low-capacity projects of varying size and type, all of which are based on the use of highly enriched fuel. One plant has been placed in operation at a remote military camp in Greenland, and another, located at Fort Greely, Alaska, is scheduled to begin operating in a few months. These projects are, however, experimental and construction and operating costs cannot yet be forecast with the accuracy necessary to permit a straightforward commercial application to a northern site. Recently, one of the smaller American projects, of a size that could conceivably have extensive application for the smaller load centres in the North and elsewhere, had a serious accident in the form of an explosion. Because this occurred in a project that is still in the laboratory stage and in the care of highly trained and experienced personnel, it suggests that we may still be some distance from the stage where only economic factors have to be considered in the applications of atomic power at more or less remote locations.

In Canada a number of studies have been undertaken in an effort to determine, with as much accuracy as available theoretical knowledge permits, the probable cost of constructing and operating an atomic energy type of power plant at some remote site. These studies have included plants fuelled with natural uranium and those requiring highly enriched fuel, with a thermal capacity ranging from two to forty megawatts and an output of electric power varying from 500 to 7,500 kilowatts. Comparisons have been made with a theoretical conventional plant supplying heat and power at a specific site. These studies indicate that in the size ranges mentioned the capital cost of a nuclear plant may be of the order of one-and-one-half to three times that of a conventional oil-fired plant of equivalent capacity, the smaller plant being more expensive relatively. There are indications that, providing the heat output of the reactor can be utilized to 60 or 70 per cent of capacity, it might be possible for some type of medium-sized atomic plant (having a thermal capacity rating of 20 to 25 megawatts) to compete on a self-liquidating commercial basis with a conventional oil-fired plant at an oil cost in the range of twenty to twenty-five cents per gallon. However, these are theoretical figures involving a certain amount of extrapolation from known equipment cost data and they assume a site where construction plant, materials, and equipment can be delivered by some form of surface transport at a similar cost for both types of plant. A detailed design for a specific case might well improve the comparison but, conversely, it might be worsened by the size and site conditions.

The characteristics of northern sites at which an atomic energy plant might conceivably be valuable may be divided into three main categories. (1) Small isolated settlements not readily supplied by surface transport, and consisting of possibly twenty or so dwellings and community buildings. The energy requirement of such a community might be expected to be of the order of fifty to one hundred kilowatts of electricity and two to three million BTU's per hour for space-heating; a reactor having a thermal capacity of 1 megawatt would probably be adequate. (2) Medium-size communities of an administrative nature with an adjacent airfield and an appreciable number of service premises and dwellings totalling one to two hundred, or larger if a military establishment is involved. Such a community might have an electric power load of one to five thousand kilowatts and a total space-heating load in the range of thirty to eighty million BTU's per hour. Atomic plants within the capacity range of 15 to 40 megawatts would be required. (3) A settlement centred on an industrial development such as mining and concentrating, and possibly metallurgical refining, probably embracing many of the features found in the second type of community mentioned. The total power and heat load of such a community might require an atomic plant having a thermal capacity in excess of 100 megawatts.

The probability of a nuclear plant being proved economic at any particular site is to a large extent dependent upon its size. In any atomic plant the energy is released in the form of heat and its conversion to electricity by means of a conventional steam turbine involves appreciable losses in the exhaust steam condensing system. It therefore follows that higher over-all efficiency will be achieved if a substantial portion of the heat output can be utilized directly, for example, for process or space-heating purposes. In communities that do not have a major industrial power load the energy requirements for space-heating greatly exceed the requirement for light and power and therefore an atomic plant as an energy source would be favoured. However, even in the North the maximum demand for space-heating exists for comparatively short periods of time and, despite the fact that heat may be required on a twelve-month basis, the annual load factor of space-heating may be as low as 50 to 60 per cent; the existence of a process-type heating load, such as digestion or drying, will, of course, improve this situation and allow greater utilization of the available capacity.

In space-heating the use of atomic energy would be predicated on a central heating system. This in turn would involve considerations of a site, in that such a system might be too costly for a spread-out community but be well suited to a closely-grouped community or one in which much of the accommodation is in apartments. Problems concerning the supply of other utility services also arise: possibly the need for a system of heated utilidors to provide protection for the water supply and sewerage lines might warrant adoption of a central heating system.

Quite apart from economic factors, considerations concerning operating problems will have an important bearing on the adoption of atomic energy in the North. One of the major problems in the commercial operation of conventional power plants is recruiting and retaining competent staff willing to reside in isolated communities, in competition with similar or more attractive opportunities afforded by the larger operations in the southern part of the country. The advent of automatic control and various self-protecting devices is, however, reducing the degree of technical competence required by the operating staff. These developments are also leading to a reduction in the numbers of the operating staff with a consequent saving in respect to supporting services such as housing, education, medical attention, food supply, recreational services, and so on. This suggests that atomic plants will have to be fully automatic and self-protecting before they will have general application in the North. It would be unrealistic to establish a nuclear plant as a commercial enterprise at a remote site if its operation were to be dependent upon an operating staff embracing more than two or three specially trained operators and technicians.

Reliability, including frequency and extent of maintenance downtime, is an important factor. It will have a direct bearing on the size and type of stand-by plant, probably of conventional nature, that would have to be provided in conjunction with an atomic plant. At the present time, costs would appear to rule out any thought of duplicating the nuclear equipment in a given plant even if the reactor elements were to be sized accordingly.

The basic problem in considering the possible application of atomic energy in the North is that there is as yet little or no experience in design, construction, and operation of a small capacity atomic plant as a commercial operation. Until such experience is acquired a number of factors will make it difficult and unwise to attempt to forecast accurately the future of atomic energy in the North. It is, however, reasonable to assume that future developments will tend to simplify current concepts or at least reduce construction and operating problems and costs. The time will no doubt come when atomic energy will be well established to meet the energy needs of the North.

One or two so-called exotic sources of energy are not without interest for the North. One of the most promising of these is the thermionic energy converter in which thermal energy is converted directly to electricity without moving parts. The device is based upon the maintenance of a thermal gradient between a hot cathode and an adjacent cool anode and the basic energy supply must therefore be in the form of heat. It is conceivable that such a converter might be employed, with a suitable reactor as the source of heat, to form an atomic power unit of low capacity but nevertheless sufficient to supply light and heat for an average dwelling. Devices of this nature are being developed in the United States for missiles. The programme includes a unit having an electrical output of thirty-five kilowatts and weighing only 1200 lb., which would be quite suitable for a small- to medium-sized dwelling. Although it may be some time before such converters emerge from the laboratory it is perhaps not too far-fetched to think that commercial production, at a cost that could be tolerated for civilian applications, is attainable.

Another source of energy is fuel cells, in which a mixture of a gaseous

fuel and air is converted by chemical processes to electricity. Fuel cells
may be developed to become an attractive alternative to the internal
combustion engine to supply small amounts of power for lighting and
domestic purposes at isolated sites. Although such a device would not
solve the problem of fuel supply because a supply of gaseous fuel
would be required, the problem might be minimized (in comparison
with petroleum products) because the fuel could be supplied and stored
under high pressure. Also, the fuel cell itself may well be more compact
and trouble-free than small internal combustion engines. The practical
application of devices such as these may yet be many years away, but
surely it is not unreasonable to think of them as complementing atomic
energy as a future source of light and heat for the more remote and isolated areas of the North.

THE LIVING RESOURCES OF
NORTHERN CANADA

M. J. Dunbar, F.R.S.C.

AT THE 1958 meeting of the Royal Society a symposium was presented
on the Potentialities of the Canadian Northwest, an area defined as
including the northern halves of the Prairie Provinces and British
Columbia, the Yukon, and the Northwest Territories west of Hudson
Bay. The present discussion is concerned only with the northern part
of this region, and with the country to the east of the area of the 1958
symposium, the eastern arctic and subarctic, in which the isotherms
sink down far to the south, and in which there is much more salt water.
"Northern Canada" is regarded as being all of the Canadian land and
sea areas north of a necessarily somewhat hazy line running through
those northern woodlands variously called "Hudsonian," "Forest Tundra
Ecotone," "Hemiarctic," and so on. It is necessary to draw the line
somewhere, because to many or most Canadians the word "north"
means everything north of Montreal, Toronto, and Vancouver, just as
to most Americans it means the whole of Canada plus the states of
Minnesota and Maine.

In the 1958 symposium, which did not give much play to marine
resources, Mr. D. B. Turner, discussing the future of the resources
of the northwest, said that "the renewable resources are the rub in
the economy. With the exception of special areas such as the Peace
River district, agriculture does not and cannot exist on a scale sufficient
to serve even light concentrations of people. Forests can and will support more people than at present but their contribution will be in
reasonably solid support of a fair number of permanent workers, not
a great addition to absolute numbers. By and large, the harvesting
of wildlife will be much as it is today and will lie mostly with native
peoples of the non-urban areas."[1] Turner gives the non-renewable

[1]D. B. Turner, "The resources future," *in* Frank H. Underhill (ed.), *The
Canadian Northwest: Its Potentialities* (Toronto: University of Toronto Press,
1959), pp. 76–89.

resources about a hundred years before they are used up, after which the northwest will decline in activity, back more or less to where it was before the present mining developments began. By that time transportation and communications will be on a much faster and larger scale than at present, so that all that would be needed in the way of permanent posts in the north would be weather stations. Let us hope that in the year 2061 there will be no more need for defence establishments.

So far as the living resources of the land are concerned, there is little doubt that Mr. Turner is right. Unless we stumble, penicillin-like, upon some wonder method of greatly increasing the rate of soil formation from rock and vegetation in the north, or find some way of defeating muskeg, tundrabog, and permafrost, the soils of northern Canada will not support even the present population, until this present ice-age is over once and for all. In northern Russia, it is reported, there have been successful attempts to develop potatoes and grain crops adapted to that climate, and to grow vegetables on a considerable scale under glass, with heating power generated from the wind. But even there the proportion of the food needed for the resident population raised in this way is quite small, and in any case the lack of glaciation in the past in that region, and the effective difference in latitude, disqualify serious comparison with northern Canada.

Nevertheless, there are things still worth trying on the land, some of which are being tried at present. A few years ago a gentleman from Germany, via Sweden, told us about his plan to grow soy bean and sunflowers on the shores of James Bay. He calculated that if the scale of production were large enough to warrant building oil-presses in the north, it would be economically rewarding to ship the oil out; we do not know how he is doing at present, but it seemed at the time a reasonable experiment to try. The raising of sheep has been much discussed, and has been tried in a very tentative way in the Fort Chimo area at the head of Ungava Bay. There are formidable obstacles to overcome, such as wolves, Eskimo dogs, and the difficulties of growing fodder, and it is not intended that the development would rival the output of Australia, New Zealand, or Scotland, but it is a long-term experiment very well worth trying for the benefit of the present local population. Unfortunately, experimental developments such as this are not kept going nearly long enough. Initial reverses and obstacles are allowed to generate despair and are taken as final negative results. It takes time, among other things, to induce hunting Eskimos to become sheep-herding Eskimos, especially if the hunting Eskimos are somewhat beaten by economic difficulties to begin with. It took two generations to establish sheep farming in Greenland, and it took almost one generation to get the cod fishery really going there, but both are successfully established today.

Dr. Leahey of the Department of Agriculture has emphasized that we need to know a great deal about arctic and subarctic soils and about the effects of permafrost on plant production before the prospects for agriculture in the north can be evaluated.[2] As he points out, this work is costly, laborious, and slow; pessimists would add that after the research is all done, anyone who has walked through the thin Hudsonian woods or over the barren grounds beyond, could lay heavy odds against the future development of prosperous farms in northern Ungava or in Baffin Island.

Wildlife of the land, as an expanding resource in the future, can almost certainly be dismissed. The considerable research effort at present going into this field is directed at the maintenance of present stocks or the rehabilitation of badly depleted stocks, and it is meeting with disheartening difficulties. It has not been possible in most cases, in any part of the world, to *increase* existing wild stocks above the natural level. Any development here, therefore, must be in the artificial production and maintenance of stocks of suitable animals by man; in other words, in domestication in the widest sense of the term. Two possibilities immediately spring to mind—the caribou (or reindeer, if you like to separate the two) and the muskox, on neither of which does the writer feel qualified to give any useful opinion. The reindeer experiment which began in 1927 has not been an outstanding success, but the reindeer are still there, now under new management, and Mr. John Teal's experiments in the domestication of the muskox have attracted great attention and lively interest.

The fresh-water resources are far from spectacular. Dr. Rawson, who was expert in this field, pointed out that, in effect, Great Slave Lake yielded the only considerable export fishery in the north (nine million pounds a year).[3] Local fisheries of size are those of the Mackenzie River and Great Bear Lake. Almost any lake in the north, of course, which has been undisturbed for decades, as many have, will offer a brief but impressive fishery, but unless it has the size of Great Slave, and is managed scientifically as Great Slave is, the story will be the same; the stock is quickly and drastically depleted, and it takes many

[2]A. Leahey, "Soil and agricultural problems in subarctic and arctic Canada," *Arctic*, 7 (1955), 249–54.

[3]D. S. Rawson, "Biological potentialities," *in* Underhill (ed.), *The Canadian Northwest: Its Potentialities*, pp. 61–75.

years to build itself up again when left alone. The trouble is twofold: low temperatures and small quantities of plant nutrients. The lakes of Canada, because they are all post-glacial, are all young, and the rate at which the phosphates and nitrates increase in concentration in them is slow; the colder the climate the slower the rate. This is especially true of lakes on the Canadian Shield. Such lakes, then, are extremely oligotrophic, and their fish populations, although they may be able to maintain some size if undisturbed, are very slow in growing; the growth rate of the individuals being cut down not only by scarcity of food but also by low temperature.

Any possible improvement in this situation, therefore, necessitates overcoming these two conditions, low plant food supply and low growth rate. The fertilization of lakes with plant nutrients has shown itself to be a delicate matter. It is very easy to over-fertilize, leading to overgrowth of plant life and the deoxygenation of the water owing to the decay of unconsumed plant matter. It is also easy to lose most of the added fertilizer through the ordinary outflow channels of the lake. But lake fertilization has been tried for the most part in temperate lakes and in lakes far older than those of northern Canada, lakes whose natural capital of nutrients was much greater to begin with. It would be well worth while to start a series of fertilization experiments on northern lakes in Canada, as a necessary preliminary to increasing the fish output. The problem of the effect of temperature on the growth of fish can then be tackled in the light of the effects of the increased food supply. It is not yet clear in any instance just what the balance of effect on growth is, as between temperature and food supply, but it should not be impossible to select fish stocks for fast growth at low temperature, given adequate food supply. In short, fish farms and fresh-water experimental stations should be established on a large scale in the north.

There have been developments in the commercial use of the arctic char, both in Frobisher Bay and in Ungava Bay, since the 1958 symposium. It is questionable whether char should be included in fresh-water resources, because the fish is anadromous and is caught at river mouths while it migrates to or from the sea. At all events, here is a significant resource which should be exploited. The yield of which the Frobisher Bay fishery is capable has been studied by Dr. Grainger and Mr. Hunter of the Arctic Unit of the Fisheries Research Board, and the work and experience of the Danes in Greenland are also available. There are char in almost every stream in the arctic; given a knowledge of the sustained yields they offer, all that is necessary to expand this industry is to ensure that it shall be mobile enough to crop many streams and that no one stream is over-fished. Arctic char are already available in restaurants in Montreal, and have been for some time. They hold well when frozen, and they are delicious, particularly when smoked; the market could no doubt absorb all that can be produced.

The native economy of the Eskimos, notwithstanding the importance of the caribou in certain localities, has been founded on the living produce of the sea; the Eskimos are essentially a coastal people. They have been, and to a great extent still are, dependent upon the sea mammals, and while the sea mammals should clearly be left severely alone for native consumption only, it is also to the sea that we, as another immigrant and successful people on this continent, must turn for the most interesting and the most hopeful possibilities in the matter of living resources in the north. The geography of the production of living stuff in the sea is a function largely of two things: light, determining the possibility of photosynthesis, and vertical stability of the upper water layers, determining the degree to which the inorganic plant nutrients are returned to the surface, to the photosynthetic zone. Of the two, the latter seems to be by far the more important. That is to say, light is everywhere available at the surface in sufficient intensity in spring and summer, and where its penetration into the surface layers is impeded by ice, and by snow on top of ice, the limiting factor still appears to be the availability of the phosphates, nitrates, and silicates. Temperature is of secondary importance here owing to the happy way in which the Q_{10} law is more honoured in the breach than the observance by the living organisms concerned.

Arctic water, originating in the Arctic Ocean, tends to be stable; in winter because the ice insulates the surface against further cooling and against wind-mixing, and in summer because the meltwater from the ice and drainage from glaciers sets up intense stratification in the salinity gradient. Considerable turbulence, resulting from storms, is necessary to upset this summer stability. Atlantic and Pacific water is much less stable in summer and very unstable in winter. Areas where arctic and non-arctic water mix (subarctic water) are also apt to be unstable, both on account of the mixing itself and on account of the concomitant atmospheric turbulence. Pure arctic water, then, is far less productive than is the water of subarctic and temperate regions, mainly owing to its greater vertical stability. We are at present only feeling towards a quantitative expression of this difference, but it is obviously very large. The standing crop of plankton in summer in West Greenland, for instance, or off the Labrador coast, is many times greater than the standing crop in the Arctic Ocean or in Lancaster Sound. In Hudson Bay, in spite of high density stratification, there are indications that the plankton production is quite large, which may tentatively be ascribed to storm turbulence in the fall of the year. In the waters of northern Canada, then, the areas of highest productivity of plankton are the Labrador Current and Labrador Sea, Ungava Bay, perhaps Hudson Bay and the waters of southeast Baffin Island, and the coastal waters off the Mackenzie area in the Beaufort Sea.

The question arises of how this plankton production relates to the production of fishes and sea mammals. The relation is not as direct as one might suppose. Both ecological and physiological factors complicate the picture. Of the factors determining the distribution of the whales in the Canadian arctic so little is known that nothing can be ventured here. For the seals and walruses it is apparent that the productivity of the water is not a limiting factor in the north. Special ecological demands apply to the several species and control the pattern of abundance and scarcity. The harbour seal needs ice-free water in winter; the ringed seal is concentrated on coastlines of complicated pattern, where the ice forms early in the fall and remains latest in the spring;[4] the walrus demands a combination of the right type of rocky shore with the presence of its molluscan food supply, and so on. Conservation of sea mammals concerns the Eskimo population primarily and there is no doubt at all that increased hunting of them would be hazardous. It would be a fine thing if the range of the walrus could be restored to its former extent, including the Labrador coast and the Gulf of St. Lawrence, but this seems too much to hope for.

Only comparatively few species of fish have overcome what seems to be a physiological barrier to success in the very cold arctic water. The result is that useful fish resources in the northern seas are restricted to the subarctic areas, the regions of the mixing of Arctic and Atlantic water, or of Arctic and Pacific water. Whether the cause of this is temperature or whether it has more to do with differences in basic productivity has not yet been settled, but present indications point to temperature. At all events, it is only beyond the southward limits of the pure Arctic water that the fishes become at all abundant either in individuals or in species. In the mixed subarctic waters of Labrador and West Greenland, there are large economically exploitable stocks of Atlantic cod, halibut, and redfish, and both regions are distinguished,

[4]I. A. McLaren, "The biology of the ringed seal (*Phoca hispoda Schreber*) in the eastern Canadian Arctic," Fish. Res. Bd., Canada, Bull. no. 118 (1958), 97 pp.

together with the waters of Newfoundland, by a great abundance of the little caplin, *Mallotus villosus*, a typical denizen of the mixed water.

Changes in the hydrographic pattern and hence in the distribution of marine life can be brought about by the action of nature and by the action of man. An example of the former is Ungava Bay, a highly sensitive area because of the delicate and apparently shifting balance that exists there between the proportions of Arctic and Atlantic water. In 1959 Le Jeune, in examining the resources of arctic char in the George River, reported that the year 1959 was abnormal in Ungava Bay in two ways.[5] It was a very heavy ice year, the pressure of ice being such that it was impossible to reach George River or Port Burwell by sea before the beginning of August, whereas both ports can usually be entered in the second half of June, from inside the bay; secondly, there appeared large quantities of caplin and of Atlantic cod (*Gadus callarias*, or *Gadus morhua*) in the interior of Ungava Bay, the former as far as the Koksoak River and the latter to the George River. The Atlantic cod is usually restricted to the region in the immediate vicinity of Port Burwell, and the caplin is normally a very rare visitor indeed. Caplin is not known to the Eskimo of the area to be present in Ungava Bay, although they have a name for it. In 1959 it formed a most important item in the diet of the arctic char, which turned from their normal crustacean food to the caplin, with the result that the colour of their flesh changed from pink to white.

Between 1947 and 1950, Fisheries Research Board parties, in four seasons, found only three specimens of caplin, young individuals taken planktonically, which may well have come from some distance outside the bay; they were not found in char stomachs, or in seal or cod stomachs.[6] In 1954 caplin was found in small numbers in the stomachs of Brünnich's murres nesting on Akpatok Island;[7] the murre is a fast flyer and could very well have taken the caplin east of Cape Chidley or across Hudson Strait, where they are known to occur.

The presence of caplin in Ungava Bay in the numbers reported by Le Jeune, and of Atlantic cod south to the George River, can probably be explained only by a change in the marine climate, an increase in the

[5]R. Le Jeune, "Rapport sur la pêcherie d'ombles chevaliers (*Salvelinus alpinus*) de Kagnerloualoudjouark (rivière Georges) pour 1959," Departement des Pêcheries, Québec (MS), pp. 67–100.

[6]M. J. Dunbar and H. H. Hildebrand, "Contribution to the study of the fishes of Ungava Bay," *J. Fish. Res. Bd. Canada*, IX (1952), 83–128.

[7]L. M. Tuck and H. J. Squires, "Food and feeding habits of Brünnich's murre (*Uria lomvia lomvia*) on Akpatok Island," *J. Fish. Res. Bd. Canada*, XII (5), 781–92.

Atlantic element in the water entering the bay. The interesting point is that caplin have been recorded at the head of Ungava Bay in great numbers on one occasion before this, in 1884, which was also apparently a time of unusually heavy ice. Lucien Turner, of the United States Corps of Signals, spent three years at Fort Chimo during and following the Polar Year Expedition of 1882. In the spring of 1884, he reported that caplin were observed in great numbers off George River, and that they could be taken in any desired numbers by hand-net at the mouth of the Koksoak River on August 8 of the same year. "This is the first instance," he wrote, "known either to whites or natives of the appearance of the Capelin in the southern portion of Ungava Bay."[8] He notes that at George River they had been seen for the first time a few years before that.

In two earlier papers the writer has suggested that a warming of the coastal waters of Labrador and Baffin Island might be expected during periods of relaxation of the intensity of the flow of Atlantic Drift water into the Arctic Ocean, for simple hydrodynamic reasons.[9] The observations by Le Jeune give force to this theory, for there is no doubt now, and there has in fact been no doubt for many years, that the warming of the marine climate in the North Atlantic Arctic, which started in the 1910's, reached its peak in the late 1930's or in the decade following, and that the recession to cooler conditions, with less intense Atlantic circulation, is now well established. Moreover, the amplitude of the ,climatic change of this present period is far greater than that in the decade of 1880 (when a transient warming was apparent in West Greenland). It may be reasonable to predict, therefore, that the warming effect in Ungava Bay and perhaps in adjacent areas will be on a more impressive scale than that of the 1880's. It is not out of the question that more Atlantic conditions may persist for a sufficient number of years to warrant the development of new fisheries there. If so, it is necessary to keep a watchful eye on hydrographic and biological events in Ungava Bay; it is unfortunate that there is already a gap in such observations since 1951.

What about the manipulation of living resources by man? For some time now, our colleagues across the Arctic Ocean have been discussing the idea of building a dam across the Bering Strait, always on the under-

[8]L. M. Turner, "Fishes," MS report, deposited with the Smithsonian Institution, Washington, D.C., and copy at McGill University, Redpath Library (1885).
[9]M. J. Dunbar, "A note on climatic change in the sea," *Arctic*, 7 (1954), 27–30, and "The present status of climatic change in the Atlantic sector of northern seas," *Trans. Roy. Soc. Canada* (Canadian Committee on Oceanography), XLIX, Series III (1955), 1–7.

standing that the building of the dam was to be followed by pumping water one way or the other through or over it. By a process of very approximate arithmetic, in which there are probably several flaws, the writer has calculated that to pump the cold Arctic layer off the Arctic Ocean, with the purpose of bringing the Atlantic water up to the surface, would take a very long time indeed, probably several tens of thousands of years, and that therefore the purpose would never be achieved because nature would more than keep up with the operation and engulf it.[10] I have found no reference in the Russian literature to the effects of building the dam as such and leaving it at that, a process that would also take time and a great deal of effort but which is not impossible; the strait is fifty miles wide and fifty metres deep. Perhaps the reason why this is not considered is that the supposed beneficial effects would be felt predominantly on the Canadian and Greenland side, not on the Siberian side.

A dam across Bering Strait would stop the inflow into the Arctic Ocean of a quantity of water from the Bering Sea which has variously been estimated as between 0.3 million cubic metres per second and 1.0 million cubic metres per second. Parenthetically, the phrase "million cubic metres per second" is very cumbersome and enters constantly into oceanographic discussion; I wish formally to propose that a new unit of water transport be adopted, one million cubic metres per second, and that it be called a "Sverdrup," after Dr. H. U. Sverdrup. Let us take it, then, for purposes of argument, that the inflow through Bering Strait is one Sverdrup. The outflow through the Strait is small and apparently intermittent, so that this is a net figure for the inflow. If this water is stopped by the proposed dam, then the *outflow* from the Arctic Ocean will be decreased by that amount.

The outflow is shared between the East Greenland Current and the Canadian Current (Baffin Island Current) approximately in the proportion of two to one, estimated at 2.90 Sverdrups for the East Greenland Current and 1.35 for the Canadian Current. Reduction in the Canadian Current by one-third of the total Arctic outflow will reduce the Canadian Current flow to one Sverdrup, or by one-quarter of its present transport. The amount of Arctic water in Baffin Bay, therefore, and especially along the southeast coast of Baffin Island, eastern Hudson Strait, Ungava Bay, and the Labrador coast, will be quite significantly reduced, and the proportion of West Greenland water in the eastern part of Hudson Strait and in the Labrador Current will be correspondingly

[10]M. J. Dunbar, "Preliminary report on the Bering Strait scheme," Northern Coordination and Research Centre, Ottawa, NCRC-60-1 (1960), 17 pp.

increased. Not only that; the proportion of Atlantic water in the West Greenland Current will also be increased. This proportion is not easy to estimate. The Irminger Current, which is Atlantic Drift water that lies outside and beneath the East Greenland Current in southeast Greenland, is very much greater in volume than the East Greenland polar water, and also very much warmer, but it is not clear how much of it forms part of the West Greenland Current once the two water masses have rounded Cape Farewell. The best guide is probably still the work of the United States Coastguard expeditions according to which the transport of the West Greenland Current at the level of Ivigtut is 7.4 Sverdrups in an average year.[11] If we assume that all the East Greenland Current is present, then it now forms about 40 per cent of the West Greenland Current. After the Bering Strait dam is built, this figure would be reduced to about 33 per cent.

These figures cannot be better than very approximate. The latest estimate of the total outflow from the Arctic Ocean is higher than the figure used here by about one-half, but if it is correct the Labrador Sea circulation has to be revised.[12] At all events, the main issue is clear: the damming of Bering Strait, without any pumping of water in either direction, would alter the marine climate of the coastal eastern arctic area quite significantly, to an extent which at present can be estimated only within wide limits. It would push the border of the subarctic mixed water zone northward into Baffin Bay and make available in Ungava Bay and southeast Baffin Island fishery resources comparable with, if not as great as, those at present found along the West Greenland coast. It would also, of course, cause a slight cooling of the coastal water of northern Alaska and the Mackenzie area, but it would not thereby remove any significant living resource.

These, then, are examples of changes in the marine productivity brought about by natural processes and, conceivably, by man. There is one marine resource in the north which could be used and which is not at present used at all, namely, plankton, both animal and plant. This suggestion has been made many times before, though not with any special reference to the north, and the problem here is technological only. Given enough pressure to use this food supply, means will eventually be found to do so.

Living resources in Arctic Canada are not abundant. The fact that,

[11]E. H. Smith, F. M. Soule, and O. Mosby, "The Marion and General Greene expeditions to Davis Strait and Labrador Sea, 1928–35," Sci. Res., Part II, Physical Oceanography (1937).

[12]V. T. Timofeyev, "Annual water balance of the Arctic Ocean, "*Priroda*, 7 (1956), 89–91 (trans. E. R. Hope, Defence Research Board, Ottawa [1960]).

in discussing their future, consideration is given to a task so Herculean as the closing of Bering Strait is perhaps indication enough that we are dealing with an economy of scarcity. But the living resources are not entirely insignificant and there are possibilities of increasing them by scientific means in the future. There is a great need for routine annual or biennial observations and measurements in northern sea waters, especially in the sensitive regions along the northern limits of the mixed subarctic water. The annual hydrographic sections now occupied under international agreement by Canada across the Labrador Current and by Denmark across the West Greenland Current should be extended northward and westward to cover Hudson Strait and the Canadian (Baffin Island) Current. Only by such constant records is it possible to keep abreast of what is actually going on.

MAN IN THE NORTH

G. Malcolm Brown

MAN IS IN MANY RESPECTS a tropical animal, and it is natural to ask if he can live in the far north. The answer is that, of course he can, if he is willing to pay the price. The price is first of all the price of the micro-climate he must take with him and in which he will largely confine himself, the price of heated shelter and clothing both in economic terms and in terms of restricted mobility and diminished dexterity. There is the price of the lack of amenities, the enforced idleness at certain periods, the loneliness of relative isolation, the inaccessibility to friends and relatives even if not isolated, and the possible disadvantages of bringing up children in the north. There is the cost of such cold exposure as cannot be avoided. Extreme cold limits the duration of work or play and it hampers activity during the shortened period. The limitation is in part the result of the discomfort which cold causes, man's tolerance of which is variable, and in part the result of the obvious fact that cold may cause actual tissue damage, as in frostbite. The limitation is also the result of the restricted ability of man to meet total body thermal stress.

The limitations that cold imposes on man may be altered favourably so that his range of activity at low ambient temperatures is increased, and the cost of arctic living thereby decreased. This statement only a few years ago provoked great controversy among physiologists, though among plain people it was thought to be quite obviously true. Much work has been done on this adjustment of the physiological response to cold but two points should be emphasized immediately. One is that the strictly physiological problems of tolerance of or acclimatization to cold are not in practice the most important problems of life in a very cold climate. The engineering and social problems of existence, though of course related, are much greater. The other point is that one can live in an arctic or subarctic climate without necessarily getting very cold, and certainly without becoming acclimatized to cold. This was nicely illustrated in a study at Churchill in which it was found that the basal metabolic rate of a truck driver increased during the winter but ten laboratory technicians showed no change.[1] However, though the physiological response to cold is not the dominant problem, full knowledge of it and of the ways it may be altered will contribute to the wisest solution of the engineering, social, and other problems which bulk larger.

ACCLIMATIZATION TO COLD

Acclimatization to cold is the sum of the physiological and biochemical adjustments which follow repeated and prolonged exposure to a cold climate. Several years ago it was suggested that it would be found that there was more than one pattern of adjustment,[2] and the evidence now shows this to be the case. In some the chief adjustment is metabolic with an increase in heat production. In others it is vascular, with cooling of peripheral tissues, the occurrence of a heat deficit, and an increase in the insulation of the homeothermic body core.

Much of the profitable work has been done on native populations in different regions, and the acclimatized Eskimos of the eastern Canadian Arctic were one of the first groups studied intensively. They have been examined with respect to their response to an acute exposure to cold and also for persistent changes between exposures to cold. An Eskimo resting in a room at 20° C dressed in clothes the approximate equivalent of 1 clo unit, that is, the rough equivalent of the clothes most of us wear indoors, is comfortable while an unacclimatized white control subject soon feels slightly cold. The rectal temperature of the two is the same and the average skin temperature of the two is the same. There are, however, notable differences in the profile of skin temperature in different regions. The Eskimo has a higher temperature on the trunk and shoulders, and temperatures on the forearm and bare hand are about 3° C lower. Muscle temperatures in the forearm, thigh, and calf are significantly lower in the Eskimo. If, however, the forearm and hand are rather heavily covered, as they must be to measure blood flow plethysmographically, the skin and tissue temperatures in forearm and hand are higher in the Eskimo, and the blood flow through both hand and forearm is 75 per cent greater. The hand blood flow in the Eskimo at 20° C is in fact what one sees in the control at 24 to 27° C.[3]

[1]A. Ames, III, and D. A. Goldthwait, "Influences of cold climate on basal metabolism," Office of the United States Quartermaster General, Military Planning Division, Research and Development Branch, Environmental Protection Series Rept. no. 136 (1948).

[2]G. M. Brown, "Cold acclimatization in Eskimo," *Arctic*, 7 (1954), 343.

[3]G. M. Brown and J. Page, "The effect of chronic exposure to cold on temperature and blood flow of the hand," *J. Appl. Physiol.*, 5 (1952), 221;

Changes in skin temperature have also been reported by those who have worked with partially acclimatized white men. Higher hand temperatures have been reported in the artificially acclimatized and seasonal changes have been seen.[4] In another experiment, a four-week bivouac in the Tyrol brought about a fall in temperature over the abdomen, back, knee, and toe, at least as measured with the face exposed to the cold.[5] A five-week bivouac in Alaska, on the other hand, caused a small but not statistically significant increase in hand temperature.[6]

The issue is confused because it is difficult to compare one experiment with another. For strict comparison, the need to know the previous exposure to cold of the subjects, the clothing at the time of the observations, and the detail of exposure is obvious. The importance of clothing and covering is illustrated by the observation that the heavily clothed hand and forearm of the acclimatized Eskimo have a temperature higher than those of unacclimatized white men, but that the reverse is true of the bare hand and the lightly clothed forearm.[7] The effect of the contemporary exposure of the face is often overlooked: the state of the peripheral vessels generally, and hence of skin and superficial tissue temperatures, is influenced by the loss of heat from the face.[8] These

G. M. Brown, J. D. Hatcher, and J. Page, "Temperature and blood flow in the forearm of the Eskimo," *J. Appl. Physiol.*, 5 (1953), 410; G. M. Brown, R. E. Semple, C. S. Lennox, G. S. Bird, C. W. Baugh, and H. C. E. Gasmann, "Physiological adjustments to acute cold exposure in Eskimos and white men," *Fed. Proc.*, 14 (1955), 322; C. W. Baugh, G. S. Bird, G. M. Brown, C. S. Lennox, and R. E. Semple, "Blood volumes of Eskimos and white men before and during acute cold stress," *J. Physiol.*, 140 (1958), 347; and G. M. Brown, R. E. Semple, C. S. Lennox, G. S. Bird, C. W. Baugh, and H. C. E. Gasmann, "Response to cold of the acclimatized Eskimo," in publication.

[4]L. D. Carlson, A. C. Young, H. L. Burns, and W. F. Quinton, "Acclimatization to cold environment; physiologic mechanisms," U.S.A.F. Tech Rept. no 6 (1951), 247; and T. R. A. Davis and D. R. Johnston, "Seasonal acclimatization to cold in man," *J. Appl. Physiol.*, 16 (1961), 231.

[5]B. Balke, H. D. Cremer, K. Kramer, and H. Reichel, "Untersuchungen zur Kälteanpassung," *Klin. Wochenschr.*, 233 (1944), 204.

[6]E. J. Heberling and T. Adams, "Relation of changing levels of physical fitness to human cold acclimatization," *J. Appl. Physiol.*, 16 (1961), 226.

[7]Brown and Page, "The effect of chronic exposure to cold on temperature and blood flow of the hand"; Brown *et al.*, "Temperature and blood flow in the forearm of the Eskimo"; Brown *et al.*, "Response to cold in the acclimatized Eskimo."

[8]A. C. Burton and G. R. MacDougall, "An analysis of the problem of protection of the aviator against cold and the testing of the insulating power of clothing," National Research Council of Canada, Rept. no. C2035 (1941); M. B. Macht and M. E. Bader, "Indirect peripheral vasodilatation produced by the warming of various body areas," Office of the United States Quartermaster General, Military Planning Division, Research and Development Branch, Environmental Protection Section Rept. no. 132 (1948).

points were illustrated in experiments by Burton and MacDougall.[9] While observing the rising average oxygen consumption and falling rectal temperatures of a group of heavily clad subjects sitting in the cold ($-14°$ C), they noted that in two members of the group, a lumberman and a truck driver, the fall in rectal temperature was very slight and the rise in oxygen consumption more prompt. Also, if air movement was fast, so that the face was cooled, Burton and MacDougall found that rectal temperatures seldom fell. These points illustrate the complexity of the temperature-regulating mechanisms and indicate that the *method* of heat loss is important as well as the *size* of the heat loss. The evidence suggests, for instance, that if peripheral tissues are kept warm, the core temperature of the body may in some circumstances fall significantly before the expected responses occur. There is other evidence to indicate that, in some persons with considerable experience of cold, a fall in rectal temperature may occur without providing the stimulus for an increase in heat production even when peripheral tissues are also cooled.[10] The point is that one must not talk simply of the effect of cold but describe the exposure to cold carefully, including in the description the area exposed and the duration, the thermal conditions of the rest of the body, and probably the previous thermal experience of the area exposed as well as that of the whole body.

The metabolic studies on the acclimatized Eskimos gave evidence of heightened thyroid activity with an increase in the serum PBI[11] and an elevation of the basal metabolic rate amounting to 29 per cent at the beginning of the summer.[12] Elevation of the basal metabolic rate has been found in white men after considerable exposure[13] but not after slight to moderate exposure. Increased tissue utilization of thyroxine has

[9]Burton and MacDougall, "An analysis of the problem of protection of the aviator against cold and the testing of the insulating power of clothing."

[10]L. Irving, K. L. Anderson, A. Bolstad, R. Elsner, J. A. Hildes, Y. Loyning, J. D. Nelms, L. J. Peyton, and D. Whaley, "Metabolism and temperature of arctic Indian men during a cold night," *J. Appl. Physiol.*, 15 (1960), 635.

[11]C. W. Gottschalk and D. S. Riggs, "Protein-bound iodine in the serum of soldiers and of Eskimos in the arctic," *J. Clin. Endocrinol.*, 12 (1952), 235.

[12]G. M. Brown, G. S. Bird, Lorna M. Boag, D. J. Delahaye, J. E. Green, J. D. Hatcher, and J. Page, "Blood volume and basal metabolic rate of Eskimos," *Metabolism*, 3 (1954), 247.

[13]A. C. Burton, J. C. Scott, B. McGlone, and H. C. Bazett, "Slow adaptations in heat exchanges of man to changed climatic conditions," *Amer. J. Physiol.*, 129 (1940), 84; L. H. Newburgh and C. R. Spealman, "Acclimatization to cold," National Research Council (United States), Division of Medical Sciences, Committee on Medical Research Rept. no. 241 (1943); S. M. Horvath, A. Freedman, and H. Golden, "Acclimatization to extreme cold," *Amer. J. Physiol.*, 150 (1947), 99.

also been reported.[14] An elevated resting metabolic rate has been reported in the arctic Indian.[15] Seasonal changes have been reported by the Japanese.[16] Elevation of the basal metabolic rate has been demonstrated repeatedly in animals by Sellers in Toronto and by Hart in Ottawa.[17] The acclimatized Eskimo also showed an increased plasma volume (with the increase amounting to as much as 40 per cent) and a lesser increase in total red cell volume, which became more nearly normal as the short summer went on.[18] Such changes in blood volume are well known in animals as the result of the work of Deb and Hart.[19] In man seasonal changes in plasma and blood volume have been noted both in temperate Philadelphia and in the colder climate of Winnipeg and the changes were in the reverse direction.[20] These changes likely represent loss of acclimatization to heat. It is probably the case that the high level of basal metabolic rate and blood volume found in the Eskimo are related. An increased blood volume is seen in patients with pathological hyperthyroidism and in these patients there is also an increased blood flow through hand and forearm as in the Eskimo.[21]

In his response to acute exposure to cold the test being immersion of the hand and forearm in a water bath at 5° C, the acclimatized Eskimo shows quite significant differences from the unacclimatized white man as exemplified by medical students and internes.[22] His rectal temperature

[14]D. E. Bass, "Cold injury," in S. M. Horvath (ed.), Transactions of the Sixth Conference, July 6–10, 1958, United States Army Medical Research Laboratory, Fort Knox, Kentucky (New York: Josiah Macy, Jr., Foundation, 1960), p. 317.

[15]Irving et al., "Metabolism and temperature of arctic Indian men during a cold night."

[16]S. Osiba, "The seasonal variation of basal metabolism and activity of thyroid gland," Jap. J. Physiol., 7 (1957), 1; and H. Yoshimura, "Seasonal changes in human body fluids," Jap. J. Physiol., 8 (1958), 165.

[17]E. A. Sellers and S. S. You, "Role of the thyroid in metabolic responses to cold environment," Amer. J. Physiol., 163 (1950), 81; and J. S. Hart, "Metabolic alterations during chronic exposure to cold," Fed. Proc., 17 (1958), 1045.

[18]Brown et al., "Blood volume and basal metabolic rate of Eskimos."

[19]C. Deb and J. S. Hart, "Hematological and body fluid during acclimation to cold environment," Can. J. Biochem., 34 (1956), 959.

[20]H. C. Bazett, F. W. Sunderman, J. Doupe, and J. C. Scott, "Climatic effects on the volume and composition of blood in man," Amer. J. Physiol., 129 (1940), 69; and J. Doupe, M. H. Ferguson, and J. A. Hildes, "Seasonal fluctuations in blood volume," Can. J. Biochem. Physiol., 35 (1957), 203.

[21]J. G. Gibson, II, and A. W. Harris, "Clinical studies of the blood volume: V. Hyperthyroidism and myxedema," J. Clin. Invest., 18 (1939), 59.

[22]Brown and Page, "The effect of chronic exposure to cold on temperature and blood flow of the hand"; Brown et al., "Temperature and blood flow in the forearm of the Eskimo"; Brown et al., "Physiological adjustments to acute cold exposure in Eskimos and white men"; Baugh et al., "Blood volumes of Eskimos and white men before and during acute cold stress"; and Brown et al., in publication.

is maintained at a higher level even though his oxygen consumption is smaller. His oxygen consumption during the actual period of exposure is the same but it is significantly less during the recovery period. His average skin temperature remains the same as the control's, but there are regional differences. The decrease in skin temperature over the extremities is slightly less than in the control, and the decrease in muscle temperatures in the arm and leg is significantly less. Nevertheless, his peripheral tissue temperatures remain lower than those of the control. At all times he maintains a greater blood flow through the exposed hand and arm as well as through unexposed extremities. Blood flow through a limb is, of course, one of the factors in the loss of heat from that limb, and it has been shown by Hildes and others that the loss of heat from the cold hand of the Eskimo is greater than that from the cold hand of a control.[23] Similar findings were reported by Irving in the case of the arctic Indian.[24] The Eskimo who had a greater plasma volume before exposure shows a greater and more rapid reduction in circulating plasma volume, but has the same urine secretion as the control. The Eskimo also shows a more rapid return to normal during the recovery period.

Very interesting comparative studies have been carried out on native populations by Scholander and Irving and their colleagues. Scholander measured oxygen consumption and peripheral skin temperatures in unacclimatized and acclimatized Norwegians during a cool night, and in Australian aborigines, who have the intriguing ability to sleep naked in very low ambient temperatures. In the unacclimatized there was restlessness and wakefulness during most of the night, a marked fall in skin temperatures of the extremities, and some increase in oxygen consumption. After several weeks, the Norwegians could sleep during the test cool night with the same scanty covering, and it was seen then that their oxygen consumption was markedly increased and they maintained the temperatures of their extremities. In contrast, the Australian aborigine tolerated a marked fall in temperature of the extremities and showed little increase in oxygen consumption.[25] These experiments illustrate two types of response to cold by the acclimatized subject. A third type has been found by Irving, Hildes, and others in the arctic Indian.[26] During a test cold night both the Indians and the controls showed increased

[23]J. A. Hildes, L. Irving, and J. S. Hart, "Some observations on the estimation of heat flow from the hands of Eskimos by calorimetry," *J. Appl. Physiol.* (in publication).

[24]R. W. Elsner, J. D. Nelms, and L. Irving, "Circulation of heat to the hands of arctic Indians," *J. Appl. Physiol.*, 15 (1960), 662.

[25]P. F. Scholander, "Studies on man exposed to cold," *Fed. Proc.*, 17 (1958), 1054.

[26]Irving *et al.*, "Metabolism and temperature of arctic Indian men during a cold night."

oxygen consumption and peripheral cooling, but the Indians, who were more comfortable and slept more, showed a decrease in body core temperature. If comparison be permitted between the results of the earlier one to two hour cold tests of the experiments with Eskimos and the results of these more recent tests extending over several hours, it can be said that the acclimatized Eskimo and the Australian aborigine are similar in that they both tolerate considerable cooling of peripheral tissues, and that the acclimatized Eskimo and the Norwegians of Scholander were somewhat alike with respect to oxygen consumption. Because the experiments were not exactly similar, strict comparison is not, however, possible.

The relevant work on white men has also varied greatly in method, but lesser oxygen consumption by the acclimatized during test exposures has been noted in two situations,[27] and increased blood flow through the fingers[28] and better maintenance of skin and rectal temperature have been found.[29] Two American workers, Heberling and Adams, have reported that rectal and skin temperatures during acute exposure to cold are better maintained in the physically fit than in the flabby, and in their experiments they did not find a statistically significant improvement in the previously fit during a prolonged winter bivouac though there was a tendency in that direction.[30] They wonder if some of the changes attributed to acclimatization to cold are not really properly attributable to physical fitness. The Eskimos studied in the experiments which have been described were fit. Some of the medical students in the control groups had done heavy manual labour during the summer; others had lifted nothing heavier than a stethoscope. There is no answer for Heberling and Adams in these experiments, but there is probably one in some of the cold room experiments where there has not been sufficient exercise to make fit the unfit, and yet altered patterns of skin temperature have been seen. It should also be remarked, apropos of the relation between skin temperature and physical fitness, that acclimatization to

[27]Carlson et al., "Acclimatization to cold environment; physiologic mechanisms"; and J. Leblanc, "Evidence and meaning of acclimatization to cold in man," J. Appl. Physiol., 9 (1956), 395.

[28]Carlson et al., "Acclimatization to cold environment; physiologic mechanisms."

[29]Horvath et al., "Acclimatization to extreme cold"; A. Ames, III, R. S. Griffith, D. A. Goldthwait, M. B. Macht, and H. S. Belding, "A study of various methods of rewarming men after exposure to extreme cold," Fed. Proc., 7 (1948), 2; E. M. Glaser, "Acclimatization to heat and cold," J. Physiol., 110 (1949), 330.

[30]Heberling and Adams, "Relation of changing levels of physical fitness to human cold acclimatization."

cold is not simply a matter of skin temperature. Two other Americans, Davis and Johnston, worked at Fort Knox, Kentucky, with a group of laboratory workers whose fitness was undescribed but may be surmised, and whose physical activity remained constant throughout the seasons concerned.[31] They found that when the technicians were placed nude in a room at 14° C for an hour in October they began to shiver at sixteen minutes, but that in February they could last almost the whole hour before shivering. Differences in skin temperature were very slight.

LOCAL TOLERANCE OF COLD

The ability of habitual outdoor workers to carry on at their tasks with bare hands in extreme cold has been remarked on both by the layman and by the physiologist. In the studies on acclimatized Eskimos ten years ago, it was noted that six of seven Eskimos who kept a hand and arm in 5 to 10° C water for two hours went to sleep after experiencing slight discomfort. The white men, on the other hand, reported sensations of severe coldness and a period of deep-seated aching pain, and none could sleep.[32] Diminished finger numbness as tested semi-objectively has been noted in outdoor workers at Churchill and in artificially acclimatized subjects at Cambridge.[33] In a Winnipeg winter, Hildes found reduced numbness in the ungloved hands as compared with the same subjects' gloved hands.[34] Hildes and others have also had a look at some Gaspé fishermen and found that their hands in cold water were less painful, had higher temperature in the fingers, and greater heat emission from the hand as a whole, as compared with the hands of others from the same community. The only difference noted on skin biopsy was an increased number of mast cells.[35] Irving found that in two students of a scantily clad religious order in Alaska, there was diminished pain sensibility when the feet were allowed to cool, but at the same time a very delicate appreciation of temperature change was maintained.[36] Some but not all of these experiments support the concept of

[31]Davis and Johnston, "Seasonal acclimatization to cold in man."

[32]G. M. Brown, G. S. Bird, T. J. Boag, Lorna M. Boag, J. D. Delahaye, J. E. Green, J. D. Hatcher, and J. Page, "The circulation in cold acclimatization," *Circulation*, 9 (1954), 813.

[33]N. H. Mackworth, "Finger numbness in very cold winds," *J. Appl. Physiol.*, 5 (1953), 533.

[34]J. A. Hildes, "Local acclimatization induced by exposure to cold," *Rev. Can. Biol.*, 16 (1957), 489.

[35]J. Leblanc, J. A. Hildes, and O. Heroux, "Tolerance of Gaspé fishermen to cold water," *J. Appl. Physiol.*, 15 (1960), 1031.

[36]L. Irving, "Human adaptation to cold," *Nature*, 185 (1960), 572.

local acclimatization without there necessarily being generalized changes. The relation between the observed greater blood flow and the increased tolerance to cold in the hand remains to be worked out.

One of the most interesting points to come out of the work on the Eskimo has been the evidence that he makes greater use of a heat exchanger which exists in the forearm and in the leg. In both the forearm and the leg the arteries are surrounded by a network of veins to an extent not seen in other parts of the body, and this makes possible an economical heat exchange between arterial blood and the cool venous blood returning from the extremity.[37] Thus, in the cold, the arterial blood reaching the hand is much cooler than it was in the arm, and venous blood reaching the body core is much warmer than when it left the hand. The pattern of tissue temperature in the forearm when the hand is warm and when the hand is cool indicates that there is greater use of this mechanism by the Eskimo and this of course makes the heat loss from his hands and feet smaller than it would otherwise be.[38] Even so, as Hildes and others have found, the loss of heat from an Eskimo's hand is larger during direct exposure to cold than that of the white controls.[39]

But how important are the modifications in loss of heat which are produced by these vascular adjustments? They may at first seem small considered simply as measures of saving heat. The loss of heat from the hands, for instance, is only a fraction of the total. Any modification of this is relatively slight compared with the total loss of heat of the body. A resting man covered with 1 clo can maintain equilibrium at 21° C and by putting on 4 clo may maintain thermal equilibrium at 0° C. For each 9° C drop in air temperature, the man dressed in 1 clo must increase his metabolism by 100 per cent. Shivering will increase it by about 300 per cent, as will a brisk walk. Though alterations of loss of heat from exposed hands may not be large as compared with changes of this size, which are events of every day life, they are important in borderline cases where their existence may prolong effective performance and they may also be important in local tolerance to cold.

[37]H. H. Pennes, "Analysis of tissue and arterial blood temperatures in the resting human forearm," *J. Appl. Physiol.*, 1 (1948), 93.

[38]Brown and Page, "The effect of chronic exposure to cold on temperature and blood flow of the hand"; Brown *et al.*, "Temperature and blood flow in the forearm of the Eskimo"; and J. Page and G. M. Brown, "Effect of heating and cooling the legs on hand and forearm blood flow in the Eskimo," *J. Appl. Physiol.*, 5 (1953), 753.

[39]Hildes *et al.*, "Some observations on the estimation of heat flow from the hands of Eskimos by calorimetry."

PROTECTION

The investigation of acclimatization to cold has been a matter of great interest, and will continue to be so. For one thing, the response to cold is a good model for the study of the control of some of the energy systems of the body. More directly, knowledge of acclimatization to cold and of its quickest method of induction may help, for instance, in determining what is the best temperature at which to keep houses in the north. Should they be kept at 15.5 to 18° C as in England, 21 to 24° C as in southern Canada, or 24 to 29° C as they often are in Churchill? However, as has been indicated already, the accomplishment of acclimatization to cold is not a great problem when one contemplates large numbers living in the north; indeed, for the great majority it will not be necessary. What will be of much greater importance is new and more effective clothing, the design of which will of course be influenced by knowledge of the physiology of cold. There is a need for the application of thin flexible materials of high insulative value which are already available and which will provide adequate protection without too much encumbrance. Tests have shown that riding a bicycle ergometer dressed in present day arctic clothing requires 10 per cent more energy than does the same task in light clothing.[40] Riding a bicycle is, however, a relatively crude task, and not one much required in the arctic cold. For other tasks involving a great variety of movements, the burden of present heavy clothing may be greater than 10 per cent, and to this must be added the loss of efficiency resulting from the restricted dexterity of those heavily bundled up. As well as having high insulative value, arctic clothing must be so arranged that it can be ventilated easily and automatically during exercise. Otherwise the subject becomes overheated, moisture accumulates, and there is trouble in the rest period following the exercise. Special gloves or mitts designed for different types of outdoor tasks are probably required, rather than one general-purpose mitt. The problem of an adequate face mask for common use has never really been settled. These examples illustrate the need for attention to the mechanics of existence in the north, if life there is not to be unnecessarily wasteful of effort.

HEALTH

Forty years ago Huntingdon showed by very detailed analysis that in tested communities in temperate climates deviations of the temperature

[40]LeB. Gray, F. C. Consolazio, and R. M. Kark, "Nutritional requirements for men at work in cold, temperate and hot environments," *J. Appl. Physiol.*, 4 (1951), 270.

and humidity from the mean for those communities were followed by increases in mortality rates.[41] This simply bore out the impression which the layman has had for a long time that wide swings of temperature take their toll. It is to be noted that these variances in mortality rate followed deviations of temperature and humidity from the means for the communities under examination. The problem can be looked at in another way. We can examine the experience of comparable populations in the arctic and in the temperate zone. The Surgeon-General of the Canadian Armed Forces has kindly provided the writer with some very interesting figures. At two large stations well in the south of Canada the average numbers of personnel off duty because of sickness each day were 5.3 and 7.5 per 1,000 strength. At a large station well in the subarctic the comparable rate was 3.9. There are special considerations such as the greater number of recent recruits at the southern stations which may explain the higher morbidity rates there. Even so, it can be taken that there is not a devastatingly higher rate of sickness in populations in northern towns. Furthermore, on examining the mortality rates in various towns in Ontario, one finds that for such towns as Timmins and Cochrane they are not significantly different from that of Chatham.[42] There are special problems of health in large communities in the north, of course, but they are not in any way insurmountable, and their presence is not so far reflected in higher morbidity or mortality rates.

Undoubtedly, a psychological and emotional problem is associated with life in the far north. Psychologists have made some interesting statements on the existence of man and his mind in strange settings. They have pointed out that, in space travel, man must arrange to take with him a segment of his physical environment and also that there must be some degree of simulation of his previous sensory environment if he is to continue to function satisfactorily.[43] This is one of the problems for those who intend to spend long times in the arctic; some of the paraphernalia of urban life in a temperate zone must be taken to the new arctic town, but exactly how much, and what, deserves a good deal of consideration. Obviously extra time, money, and effort must be spent on providing communication through different media so that the difference in this respect between Frobisher Bay and Kapuskasing becomes something of the same order as that between Kapuskasing and Toronto or Montreal.

[41]E. Huntingdon, *World Power and Evolution* (New Haven, Conn.: Yale University Press, 1919).

[42]*Vital Statistics for 1959 for Ontario* (Ottawa: Queen's Printer, 1960).

[43]D. O. Hebb, "The mammal and his environment," *Amer. J. Psychiatry*, 111 (1954), 826, and "The role of experience," in publication.

One of the standard authors of the day has stated that man needs the spur of a continual stimulus from his environment to reach his full powers. According to this theory, the stimulus must be adequate to call forth his energies, but not so great that the majority of his time and activity is taken up in dealing with it. As far as life in the arctic is concerned, the stimulus is the need to adjust to its particular environment. As we have seen, there is no great medical or physiological obstacle to life in the north. The real problem is one of economic adjustment. Such adjustment is quite within the possibility of accomplishment and life in the arctic may be so arranged that it is productive and stimulating. If the adjustment were well made it is even possible that arctic communities would provide a most satisfactory setting for the full growth of man.

THE FUTURE COLONIZATION OF
NORTHERN CANADA

Trevor Lloyd

WHEN SEEKING TO DRAW CONCLUSIONS concerning the large-scale colonization of northern Canada it is important to keep in mind the extent and character of the region we are discussing. The North is vast in area, just how vast it is not easy to appreciate unless one has travelled it on the ground as did Camsell, Tyrrell, and Low and not a few veteran Fellows of the Royal Society of Canada. Its scale may be illustrated by a circle centred on Montreal and passing through Alert at the northern end of Ellesmere Island. It also passes through the delta of the Mackenzie River, cuts the Pacific well to the west of Vancouver Island then touching San Francisco, Trinidad and Iceland. Those geometrically minded may care to remember that an approximate equilateral triangle can be formed by joining Vancouver, the Bay of Fundy and Alert, N.W.T.; the sides of the triangle would be approximately 2,500 miles long.

PHYSICAL CHARACTER

In character, the enormous land mass of northern Canada is, as has been shown earlier in this volume, diverse. It may be usefully divided into regions based on the nature of its bedrock types and their surface manifestations. In some areas the landforms were recently modified by glaciation and a few higher parts are still beneath the ice. Within the one-and-a-half million square miles of northern Canada lies scenery as diverse as are the Rockies and the western plains, the Laurentians and the St. Lawrence lowland, the sandy beaches of Prince Edward Island and the fjords of British Columbia.

The climate is almost equally varied. This is a consequence of the interrelated influence of latitude and elevation, and of location with respect to oceans, seas and other land masses. A map of natural vegetation emphasizes the striking distinction between east and west. Thus, the treeline, significant as an indicator of summer temperatures, and also of great ecological and economic importance, reaches north of 68° N. Lat. in the Mackenzie Valley, but on the Labrador coast lies south of the 55th parallel, a difference of a thousand miles. The soils, which have been dismissed rather cavalierly by some, may, it is true, be of limited extent and fertility but in a few areas, particularly the northwest, are of real local significance. The seas, a major topic for study in themselves and one all too long neglected in Canada, serve both as a reservoir of food and as a means of travel, though obstructed by ice for much of the year.

On the basis of these and other physical characteristics, the Canadian North is divisible into five main regions—the mountain ranges and plateaus characterized by much of Yukon; the Mackenzie Valley; the mainland area extending from Churchill northward and westward to the seacoast, devoid of trees, with severe winters and short cool summers, and underlain by Precambrian rocks; a fourth region from New Quebec northward to Lancaster Sound, loosely termed the Eastern Arctic; and to the far north the fifth, which includes the Arctic islands. In physical characteristics and the means needed for development, each of the five regions has within itself a certain degree of unity. An important physical characteristic lacking in southern Canada but widespread in the North is perennially frozen ground, the so-called "permafrost." New to engineers, miners and community planners, its presence must be taken seriously if disaster is to be avoided.

Such then is the background against which human activities in the Canadian North must be considered.

TRANSPORTATION

It is universally recognized that efficient and economical transportation holds the key to much of northern development. So it may be useful to recall the main lines of communication between the settled areas of southern Canada and the Far North. For ocean-going vessels there are two main routes: the lesser is based on coastal British Columbia and passes around Alaska into the western Arctic, a frequently hazardous route; the other is based on the St. Lawrence region or the Maritimes and passes northward to enter Hudson Bay or continue through Davis Strait to the Arctic islands. The "Northwest Passage" famous in history is not significant as a "through" route although parts of it are used regularly. Hudson Bay, Baffin Bay, and the western Arctic coast are readily navigable in most summers, but sea-ice conditions vary from year to year. No part of the Canadian North is as favoured as is West Greenland south of the Arctic Circle where navigation is possible all year.

The Canadian railway network sends lines northward at several points, the two most significant being those based on Edmonton and tapping the Mackenzie Valley, and that based on southern Saskatchewan and reaching eventually to Churchill on Hudson Bay. Two highways are similarly significant, the one leading from Edmonton to Alaska by way of Yukon and the other reaching the Mackenzie Valley at Great Slave Lake and recently continued to Yellowknife.

The pattern of commercial air routes is very similar. An eastern "flyway" extends to Frobisher on southern Baffin Island, a central one by way of Churchill penetrates to Resolute Bay and thence to the Arctic islands, while a third route from Edmonton follows the Mackenzie Waterway to the coast. The Yukon is served by a route roughly paralleling the Alaska Highway.

POPULATION

By customary standards the total population of northern Canada is negligible. There are a few pockets of concentration, some areas where semi-nomads roam, and a vast area with no-one at all. Yukon, a relatively populous area, has fifteen square miles for each person. The Mackenzie District, with an area of half a million square miles, provides a home for only 14,400 people, or thirty-five square miles for each one. North of the treeline each person has about seventy-six square miles.

Apart from the native Eskimos and Indians, most of the residents retain close ties with "the outside," being in the North for a more or less brief tour of duty and, even if settled there, looking to the south for supplies and periodical refreshers. The Indian and Eskimo populations are small in number. Until the 1941 census, the total was not known with even fair accuracy. It is a measure of the improved administration of northern affairs that the modern census combined with "family allowance" records provides today a reasonably true picture of Eskimo numbers and distribution. The population is rising, health is improving (the death rate from tuberculosis dropped to one-seventh in the last ten-year period) and infant mortality is declining. In fact, a coming population bulge is a new and unexpected hazard facing administrators.

Small though the northern population is, it includes diverse groups, ranging from exiled city dwellers, haunted by all the problems of suburbia, to semi-nomadic hunters not far removed from the Stone Age. So when considering the problems of northern development, along with the diversity of physical geography, account must also be taken of the wide gulfs that separate northern residents. To grant "self-government" to such a region may in fact mean to place the economic future of native Eskimos and Indians in the hands of white residents such as miners and traders.

SOVEREIGNTY

Occasionally one still hears of uncertainty about Canada's sovereignty over the Arctic. While there may at one time have been grounds for doubt concerning the effectiveness of this country's title to all its Arctic possessions, and there may even have been some fear that parts might be lost by default, there is no such risk today. Canada's title is universally recognized. The area of national responsibility was increased recently when the right to extract minerals from the submerged Continental Shelf was internationally recognized. This explains in part the present hurried search to locate the outer limit of the Shelf lying north of the Queen Elizabeth Islands.

DEVELOPMENT COMPARED

The complaint is often heard that northern Canada has been neglected and that its development has proceeded slowly in comparison with Greenland, northern Scandinavia, or the Soviet Union. Such comparisons may be misleading, particularly because they seldom take account of significant differences in the physical characteristics of the several areas. An obvious case of this is the frequently contrasted development of the Canadian Eastern Arctic and Danish West Greenland, on the other side of Davis Strait. Along the Greenland coast between Cape Farewell and Melville Bay is a string of large and small communities certainly not duplicated across the water in Canada. There is, however, a fundamental difference in physical geography between the two areas, based primarily on climate supplemented by the influence of nearby waters. It is this that makes possible the plan to export Ungava iron ore by way of an ice-free transit harbour on the Greenland coast. West coasts are always milder than east coasts in high latitudes, as is apparent from a comparison of the climates of Norway and Pacific U.S.S.R., or the Alaskan Panhandle and Labrador. Thus Murmansk in northwestern U.S.S.R., with a population of a quarter of a million, is at a latitude approximating that of the coast of the Canadian Arctic mainland. But the climates are entirely different. Other contrasts between physical conditions in northern Canada and those in northern U.S.S.R. are apparent when one compares the extent of territory which lies north of the treeline in both cases. The Canadian area is far more extensive and complex, and there are other important distinctions. Nevertheless, some useful circumpolar comparisons may fairly be made. The large river valleys flowing northward to the Arctic Sea are a case in point. In Canada the Mackenzie, together with its tributaries, is located much as are the Lena, the Yenesei, and the Ob of Siberia. All of these rivers are used by shipping that links the railroad systems of the South with the Arctic Sea coast. There is no doubt that the tonnage of freight moved on the Mackenzie does not compare with that on the Siberian rivers. The difference gives some indication of the relative development of the two areas. There is nothing in Canada to compare with the mining city of Norilsk, where over 100,000 people live at almost 70° N. Lat. some miles east of the Yenesei.

One great and unique physical asset Canada does have in the North. This is Hudson Bay, a gateway to the heart of North America. That it has been utilized far less than it might have been in the past thirty years is a fair commentary on Canada's attitude towards northern expansion.

THE ECONOMIC BASIS FOR CANADIAN ARCTIC SETTLEMENT

There appears to be a widely held view that the primary purpose of developing northern Canada is to supply raw materials needed by southern industries or, if these are adequately served from elsewhere, to secure foreign exchange by exporting the resources. The future of the North is thus seen as that of an economic colony of the already industrialized South. My own view, expressed often in the past, is that this provides no basis for a permanent northern population. Such can only come about if a reasonably self-contained society can be established there. In any event, there is little in contributions to this symposium to encourage those who await impatiently a far northern industrial boom. Information provided about the economics of northern mineral exploitation suggests that it may be a very long time indeed before large-scale mining operations are likely, except possibly in a few favoured and strategically placed locations. The obvious lack of enthusiasm shown by southern industry for venturing into the Far North is not peculiar to Canada. It seems to be universal along the northern frontier. Since the state trading monopoly in Greenland was lifted a decade ago there has been no appreciable rush of private capital anxious for investment there. So too elsewhere in Scandinavia. A Norwegian businessman at Hammerfest, one of the most northerly cities in the world, told me recently that "Bankers don't lend money north of Trondheim" (a city which lies one-third of the way up the long Norwegian coast). And even in the Soviet Union it is now authoritatively reported that "economic laws" govern the exploitation of Arctic resources. This is revealed in a recent paper on the economics of Soviet Arctic development, which states:

The development of natural resources will be economically expedient only under two conditions.
1. When the special value of these resources justifies the high outlays necessary.
2. When the resources in question are generally scarce in the country and their development is essential for the pressing needs of the national economy and for strengthening the country's military preparedness.[1]

If a considerable population is to be settled in the Canadian north-land, what resources are likely to be available to attract it and support it?

Lumber is far from negligible—at least in the Yukon and the Mackenzie Valley—and is likely to prove adequate for all local needs. About one hundred million board feet per annum are available for cutting in the Yukon, while less than one-twentieth of this is at present used.[2]

Agricultural lands are not to be overlooked, particularly in areas where urban centres grow up and there is a demand for fresh vegetables, milk, and eggs. Land awaits use in the Yukon and Mackenzie Valley every bit as good as that now being broken for new settlers in northern Finland and Norway. There are believed to be a quarter of a million acres of arable land available in Yukon and five times that amount in the Mackenzie Valley.[3] Persons familiar with the area can vouch for the usefulness of the small-scale farming operation long carried on there and now encouraged by agricultural research stations. Of course, when the soils and the climate are compared with those of more smiling lands they are not impressive but they are still capable of making life healthier, pleasanter, and less expensive for those who must live there. Where local coal, oil, or natural gas exist, hothouse cultivation of vegetables could be undertaken.

---

[1]S. V. Slavin, "Management of the Socialist Development of the Soviet North: Methods and Forms," *in Problems of the North* (Ottawa: National Research Council, 1960), pp. 247–62. (Translation of *Problemi Severa*, no. 1 [Academy of Sciences of the U.S.S.R., 1958].)

[2]B. G. Sivertz, "The North as a Region," *Resources for Tomorrow* (Ottawa, 1961), I, 571.

[3]*Ibid.*, p. 569.

There has been earlier mention of the fish resources of lakes and seas.[4] While these may, in a few cases, be able to serve the luxury markets of New York, Chicago, and Montreal, they may elsewhere be an important source of food for the local population.

However, today—as almost fifty years ago when Charles Camsell first wrote about it[5]—the development of the Far North is generally considered to depend upon the exploitation of minerals. It is for this reason that the contribution by Henderson and Buck is included in this symposium. The magic of the Precambrian Shield and of the oil and gas presumably hidden in the strata to its west and north, is the basis for most of the hopeful forecasting about the future of the North. Yet the record as seen today is not impressive. We are still far from being able to justify, on the basis of returns from minerals produced there, the large public investment made in northern Canada. Gross revenues from minerals amount to about twenty-three million dollars a year for the Northwest Territories and twelve million dollars from the Yukon, and the amount has fallen in recent years. The publicly owned mining operation on Great Bear Lake has, perhaps conveniently for some critics, ended with the petering out of the ore supply, and the company has agreed to give up the search for more. A small nickel mine on the west coast of Hudson Bay may prove to have had only a brief, if meteoric, career. There are no other truly arctic mines in Canada. In the Northwest Territories there remains only the Yellowknife area to demonstrate what mining can do for northern development after forty years of intensive effort. The small oilfield at Norman Wells, first detected fifty years ago, is now used to barely half of its capacity and is the lone producer in northern Canada. The vast flow of petroleum products which constantly pour northward at enormous cost for freight and non-returnable oildrums originates on the Prairies or in Venezuela and the Near East. When given the "cold, hard look" customary in trade and commerce, the mining industry of northern Canada today, despite the large sums and enormous effort spent on it, offers a singularly fragile foundation on which to build a new northern empire.

In striking contrast, there can be no doubt that one public agency has been notably productive as a basis for arctic development both in Alaska and Canada. I refer of course to defence enterprises. These alone have commanded the public financial resources, the priorities,

[4]See M. J. Dunbar, "The Living Resources of Northern Canada," in *Canadian Population and Northern Colonization*, Royal Society of Canada "Studia Varia" series (Toronto: University of Toronto Press, 1962), pp. 127–37.

[5]Charles Camsell, "The Unexplored Area of Continental Canada," *Geog. J.* (Sept., 1916), pp. 249–57.

and the technical knowledge to achieve more northern development in a decade than had seemed likely in a century. From Northeast Greenland to the outermost Aleutians there are now well-equipped settlements, provided with first-class communications, often with year-round airfields and in many cases with access by sea. A remarkable concentration of scientific expertise and industrial "know-how" has gone into their location, construction, and maintenance. The personnel occupying them are not only highly trained in their special skills but in some cases have become expert at working under arctic conditions.[6]

Much though one may regret the reasons for its being there, and deplore the enormous cost to the community, it remains true that without the DEW line and associated development the hope of effective occupation of the Far North would be even more remote today than it is. Such far-ranging enterprises have made possible elaborate programmes of research and development which have speeded the solution of many problems in logistics, housing, and communication. When the military men eventually evacuate their settlements, as is beginning to happen at some arctic sites, they will leave behind them an invaluable group of well-endowed oases in the northern wilderness.

SETTLEMENT OF THE FAR NORTH

This brings us to the fundamental question—what kind of settlement or type of colonization of the Far North is desirable and also possible? In answering this I shall repeat views I have expressed elsewhere, reinforced by the contributions of other authors of this study.

1. There is not likely to be in the near future a large movement of permanent settlers to the North. The present resident labour force there totals about 8,500 men, and is likely to increase to about 14,500 in the next decade.[7] Sufficient employment at a living wage for this group is not now available. As standards of health rise, as a result of better social services, northern Canada will presumably become a labour surplus area. The first obligation on the authorities is to provide the Eskimos and Indians with useful occupations in the part of Canada where they choose to live. This is presumably the main reason for the present drive to educate northerners, to provide many of them with economically useful technical skills, and also to help those not capable of such a revolutionary change to maintain themselves by traditional occupations supple-

---

[6]The United States Air Force base at Thule, Greenland, is in effect a city devoted to defence operations based largely on scientific research and development.
[7]Sivertz, "The North as a Region," p. 576.

mented by small-scale craft industries. In the absence of the kind of profit enterprises common in the south, co-operatives and other modest community ventures are being encouraged to make possible development of local resources as, for example, the fish and timber of Ungava Bay.

2. The possibility of developing northern minerals on a commercial scale lies in a co-partnership of private industry (if it desires to participate) and public enterprise. This has been demonstrated in other arctic areas of the world (a Canadian mining company has shared in a Greenland government mining project and a Canadian airline may adopt a similar technique there). Such "joint operations" are far from impossible in northern Canada, because there is a long tradition of comparable public enterprise in the provinces. However, in the case of mining it has become customary for public funds to be expended by subsidies or other devices without in return retaining a share in title to the industry. In this matter other nations such as Denmark, Norway, Sweden, and Finland appear to be more hard-headed, seeing to it that the capital invested by the state also earns its share of the profits (as it bears a proportion of the losses) along with private capital.[8] Cases have been cited of mining industries in the Canadian northwest where the contribution from public funds has been or may be expected to be very high indeed. The railway to Great Slave Lake to be built with public funds is likely to cost far more than the mine it is designed to serve. There would seem to be sound reasons to ensure that the public interest will be protected by joint ownership of such enterprises. Some might consider that Canada should go even further, and enable the state itself to take the initiative in determining *when* a valuable national resource should be developed. A case in point might be the valuable lead and zinc deposit on Great Slave Lake, which will apparently continue to lie idle until the smelters at Trail, B.C., need concentrates to keep them going. On such a basis, any ores, oil, or gas there may be in the north will continue to serve as a "strategic reserve" to be called on when thought appropriate in London, New York, or the Hague. This would seem to be a less than satisfactory way for Canada to develop its resources and to people its frontiers.

3. Since rapid development of the Far North based on mineral resources is not to be expected in the near future, there is still time to ensure that when such development does take place, it will be rational,

[8]A recent Canadian recognition of this need may be cited from the Province of Quebec. See interview with Premier Jean Lesage concerning provincial financial collaboration in developing natural resources, *Montreal Star*, Sept. 1, 1961.

and in the best interest of the country as a whole. The time made available to us should therefore be utilized in such ways as these:

(*a*) To explore and study the Canadian North thoroughly to determine with reasonable accuracy its extent and main characteristics, in other words "to map it" scientifically (on a scale of about four miles to the inch), to show bedrock geology, terrain types, forests, soils, and biological resources. Such an inventory-taking can be carried out far more speedily today than was possible even a decade ago, and particularly in the 1920's and 1930's when a similar undertaking was initiated in the Soviet Union.

(*b*) To provide, at strategic locations in the North, a network of permanently-manned scientific stations for regular observation of the various geophysical phenomena and to serve as bases for the scientific study of surrounding areas.

(*c*) To initiate a long-term, systematic study of all aspects of the arctic seas, including the Polar Basin. Little has been done as yet by Canada along these lines. There is still only very limited knowledge of sea-ice conditions, for example, vital though this is to secure and dependable navigation.

(*d*) To undertake long overdue social and economic studies related to development of the natural and human resources of the North. Success or failure of settlement there may well depend upon them.

A large-scale scientific stocktaking of northern Canada of the kind envisaged here will be very expensive. There can be no place in it for waste, or for duplication of effort. There will need to be genuine co-ordination, a balancing of work between the traditional scientific disciplines and an absence of inter-departmental rivalries in government agencies. An expansion of the co-operative system being tested by the Polar Continental Shelf Project would seem to have much merit.

So pressing is the need for scientific activity in the north that all available means should be employed. Generous help should be provided from public funds for the universities and for such private agencies as the Arctic Institute of North America. This is essential, not only to speed the work itself but also to ensure production of the new generation of arctic scientists and administrators so urgently needed.

Some developments in northern Canada cannot, however, await completion of this gigantic scientific stocktaking, for economic and social improvement is long overdue. When planning new industries, better communities, modern transportation, and greater use of the local resources, the authorities will need to take into account the following:

(i) The rôle of the native people should be paramount. They have been dispossessed of their inheritance without fair compensation, and are entitled to adequate education and training to allow them to play eventually a leading part in their native land. My own view is that Canada should follow a policy of absorbing the Eskimos and Indians, at present isolated from other Canadians, into the general community. There is no need for compulsion in this; there are many examples from other lands of the effectiveness of equality of opportunity in education and employment for bringing it about. There is, however, much lost ground to be retrieved. At Canadian universities one is aware of the presence of peoples welcomed from many a distant, under-developed land. I have, however, yet to encounter many students from the not-so-distant under-developed territory of Caughnawaga or the remoter colony of Pangnirtung.

(ii) The wildlife and other renewable resources must be carefully preserved for posterity.

(iii) Strict control over non-renewable resources should be retained for the benefit of the community as a whole, and not alienated for the short-term enrichment of speculators, Canadian or not.

(iv) No appreciable development of the Far North is likely without large public investment, whether in scientific surveys or for construction of harbours, airfields, radio aids, roads, railways, towns, schools, and churches. This enormous investment of public funds will surely need to be safeguarded. It seems to me incontrovertible that the common good requires that companies operating in the Far North must include an appreciable proportion of public capital in their financial structure. Such may, in fact, be the only way of ensuring that control over company policies is employed in the interest of this country.

Nothing I have said suggests that the immediate future of the Canadian north is a particularly rosy one. Large outlays must be anticipated before there is much income, for the road to national development is always expensive. All we can determine at present is that the resources that may exist in the North will be wisely utilized, that the local residents shall not be exploited, and that planning for the future must be based on a broad, systematic, and thorough scientific appraisal.